The Adolescent

The
ADOLESCENT

by

MARYNIA F. FARNHAM, M.D.

HARPER & BROTHERS PUBLISHERS

New York

1952

TO LINDA AND LEDA

who sometimes sat for the portrait

Contents

Contents

Introduction

This book sets out to describe and explain the inner workings of boys and girls in their teens—adolescents. As a group these young people seem to be out of gear with the rest of society. They have become a problem. By some, they are listed as the Number One problem; indeed to many people, adolescence is almost synonymous with delinquency. Few adults seem to feel comfortable or competent where these youngsters are concerned. Many parents look forward to the age with grim foreboding, bracing themselves for the shock, expecting the worst. Apparently they feel that arrival at the teens means that the boy or girl is going automatically to break out into strange excesses of behavior and become progressively less understandable and manageable. Too often they seem willing to throw in the towel and turn the whole thing over to the child, chance, or the ministrations of schools and other agencies.

There must be some reason why this time of life—a natural and inevitable period in development, often full of charm and beauty—should have become a major mystery. Has there been some essential change in the nature of the adolescent? That seems hardly likely. What is true is that there has been great change in the social situation in which adolescence is acted out. This change is apparent in every phase of the young person's life. The family has changed. The economic surroundings have changed. The social organization has changed from one largely rural to one that is largely urban. The length of time during which the individual is dependent has been prolonged. The mores have changed and are still in the process of changing. A development that is consistent with the earlier forms of society can easily be out of gear in a changed form.

To be sure, adolescents are not the only people who are bewildered and disturbed today. The adults around them are forced to cope with the problems that they are only beginning to face. If these growing youngsters, who appear to require so much attention and to pose so many problems, are to be dealt with properly and prevented from endangering themselves in this complex society, it is necessary to understand the forces that are operating within it. Time was when everything seemed to happen naturally and there was no need for any particular orientation on the rearing of children. That time has passed. We are now in a period when the complexities of life require the greatest possible understanding from anyone who wishes to be a successful parent.

Most young people, or at least a great many of them, manage to grow up without running into special difficulties. The process is natural and inevitable, and on the surface there seems no reason why it should be unduly complicated. Most parents want to see their youngsters develop in the ways that will make them happy and comfortable. The vagaries and natural but special characteristics of this age are taken in stride by a great many parents. This is easier to do if the earlier years have gone smoothly. But even in this happy circumstance, there are many signs that adolescence is a time of life that can take a good deal of understanding. There is some important evidence that during these years youngsters are particularly prone to get out of kilter. At one time or another there is apt to be a troublesome spot. It is a happy parent indeed who never finds anything to puzzle and worry him about the growing-up process of his youngsters.

For that reason it seems useful to try to put down, as simply as possible, a description of the mechanics of adolescence and the way in which these processes express themselves. This will include a description of the changes that are to be expected and of the forces behind them. The youngster will be described in all his various phases: physical, emotional, intellectual, social and sexual. The way in which these changes manifest themselves will be described. The meaning of the behavior of young people in relation to themselves, their families and their associates, and the relation of their behavior to the forces with which they are dealing will be considered. Some of the misfortunes and failures of development will be discussed and interpreted. Finally, we will try to relate all this to the pressures around the adolescent and to point out how the attitudes of society and of the parents play into the difficulties that are encountered. How we as parents, the products and representatives of society, are failing to meet the basic needs of these young people and how we can better learn to help them deal with the problems of this time of life and come to a happy maturity, is really our main consideration.

The Adolescent

The Physical Process

Everyone knows an adolescent by looking at him. He isn't grown up. Neither is he a child. He is not at all of a piece. There is a subtle emanation from this youngster which everyone recognizes—a delicacy, a tenderness of structure and manner, an air of alertness and wonderment, which are signally the quality of youth.

The elemental fact behind the general impression he gives is the great phenomenon of growth. All of a sudden, after a rather quiet period, the child begins to shoot up so markedly that everyone knows the process has begun. This growth isn't new. The central fact of a child's life from his birth to his maturity is growth. But his early growth is a regular and orderly process compared to the growth that starts with the beginning of puberty. Before, there has been only an increase of size without any essential change in the quality of the body form, which continues to appear childlike. Changes are, of course, going on. But they do not alter the essential form. The harmonious and charming figure is still that of a child.

With the onset of puberty all this changes. Not only does the child increase greatly in over-all size but the relationships of various parts of the body to each other change, too. The first tendency is toward a thickening process. Weight increases; there is more of it altogether. This increase in bulk is rather precise and has been calculated and measured in its particulars, but those are details that need not concern us here. The increase comes from a growth in the length of the bones and an expansion in the size of the muscles. There is a great lengthening in the bones of the arms and legs in particular; they grow faster than the rest of the body and are not always matched in development by the muscles. This fact accounts for the impression that most youngsters give at one time or another of being all arms and legs. The coltish, gawky effect is so typical of this age that it is almost a trade-mark.

But this is only the beginning. The body cage enlarges and both the hip girdle and the chest show signs of thickening. They broaden and deepen and change in configuration and pitch in relation to the rest of the body. The chest enlarges from front to back, and its capacity is greater than in childhood. The pelvic cavity, the bony cradle that houses the organs of generation in women, and the bladder and lower bowel in both sexes, begins to take on its final form. In girls, this means a deepening and widening as well as a flaring outward at the upper edge. At the same time the whole pelvis tips forward on its axis so that the external genitalia are now more concealed within the wall formed by the thighs. The entire girdle area becomes heavier and there is some fat deposit in the buttocks and thighs. The boy, too, shows typical changes. His girdle area becomes narrowed and powerful so that eventually he acquires the small-hipped, broad-shouldered outline characteristic of the male. His whole musculature is heavier and harder and stronger where the girl's is round and soft. The net result of the changes in bone and muscle is the gradual formation of a body that is definitely masculine or feminine. The one bespeaks driving power, the other abiding strength.

The spurt in growth does not take place at the same age in all children. Some youngsters of fourteen, for example, will remain small and childlike while others will by then have done a prodigious amount of growing and have all the earmarks of the early adolescent. This is unimportant in terms of the child's physical development, unless there is a really exaggerated delay, but the child himself may not look at it that way. Children don't like difference. The boy or girl who varies noticeably from the group with which he is associated may be temporarily thrown out of joint in his social relations; and the very small boy of fourteen is in just as bad a case as the enormously tall boy of twelve. In both instances he feels out of his group and uncertain of himself. He is threatened in one of his most important sources of security, his sense of belonging. Generally speaking, one finds it easy to be comfortable in a group made up of similar individuals. But the strange, the exotic, the extraordinary all threaten the solidarity of the group, and the individual who becomes markedly different is likely to find himself on the outside, rejected and isolated.

A youngster in this situation was brought for examination because he was inattentive in school, often quite insolent and difficult to manage. He was bright enough by all tests, and was quite able to do his work when he put his mind to it, which most of the time he failed to do. Punishment had not the slightest effect on him and he seemed almost blandly indifferent to his teachers' and parents' frantic attempts to make him conform. One glance at him gave a pointer at least. He was a small, almost birdlike boy who looked ridiculous in the long trousers and bow tie which his associates were wearing and which he, too, insisted upon wearing. He was talkative and apparently self-assured. When he was examined, it was found that he was markedly undersized and his large parents were chagrined and unhappy about it. Treatment soon showed that he felt so small, so unimportant and so unmanly that he was almost overcome by the realities of the schoolroom and the playground. He either escaped into daydreams where he was always a large and powerful man, or denied his plight by insolent boldness which seemed to him a substitute for manly size.

There are all sorts of deviations and temporary derangements. Sometimes there is a tendency to very decided under- or overweight. Overweight seems to present a greater social problem. Girls, particularly, are likely to regard such a condition as a catastrophe. No one is allowed to be fat today and have any claim to attractiveness. So says Hollywood, the advertising fraternity, the woman's magazine—so says society. The girl who cannot find clothes to fit her feels herself a pariah. It is fashionable to look for some glandular defect or disturbance when there is a noticeable tendency to overweight but this is seldom the root of the trouble. Usually, diet will be found to be responsible for the difficulty and generally the child will outgrow it.

Worse still does it seem if some particular part of the body is not of a size or form regarded as suitable. For girls, this means breasts and hips. They must be neither too large nor too small. For boys it means height and shape and size of the body as well as the size of the genital organs. Some boys will for a time at this age take on an appearance of girlishness, with rounded smooth contours, rather large hips and soft skin. (The girl may fail to develop typical female contours and look rather boyish.) Only a few such children have any real physical problem; usually the body takes on a typical form within a relatively short time. If the condition is greatly exaggerated or much prolonged, the youngster should be seen by a doctor.

Some skin changes are normal to the growth situation. A general thickening of skin texture is expected. The appearance of body hair in typical sexual distribution is noticed quite early and is of concern to both boys and girls. Anxious anticipation of a beard which will be sufficiently imposing to justify the use of a razor is a regular part of the healthy boy's reaction to his changing body. Again, there are deviations. Especially disturbing to girls is a tendency to hairiness on the face or any place where it is associated with masculinity. Typically, the sites for excess hair growth in girls are the face, between the breasts, around the nipples and in the center line of the abdomen. It is obvious that these are the areas that are typically hairy in men. Naturally any girl is going to be worried about such variations from what she has been taught to expect.

The problem should be dealt with very carefully and exactly. It can't be brushed aside or neglected. Hair on a girl's face is a blemish and nothing that anyone can say is going to change that. There may be a notion that this is a difficulty associated with improper functioning of the glands, and so it may be. But much more likely it is one that cannot be dealt with by any glandular injection or treatment. The first thing to do is to find out by consulting the family doctor. If he says (as he very likely will) that there isn't anything medical to be done, the only treatment for any heavy growth is removal by the electric needle. If there is only a very slight growth around the nipples or between the breasts, it can be disregarded unless the girl is too disturbed by it. A fine line of hair on the mid-line of the lower abdomen never seems to arouse any particular feeling. Hair on the arms or legs is easily dealt with.

Another skin change of great importance is in the sweat glands. There is an absolute increase in the quantity of sweat secreted, and a change in its nature. Everyone is aware that children, no matter how hot or dirty, never smell offensive. This is because the part of the sweat glands that gives perspiration its characteristic odor remains inactive until puberty. Nowadays, body odors are not tolerated, and many youngsters are brought face to face with this fact in ways that are all too lacerating. One little girl was heartbroken to be told by her schoolmates to "go home, take a bath and put on Odorono." Specific instruction in personal hygiene will prevent such little tragedies. If, at first, the skin reaction prevents using standard antiperspirants, deodorants will do the trick.

These are natural changes to which everyone expects to adjust. But there are some fairly frequent skin disturbances that are more distressing because they are felt to be unattractive. The skin eruption, acne, for example is so common that it can almost be considered a usual part of the adolescent picture. The skin, becoming overactive, secretes oily substances faster than they can be carried off; they therefore accumulate in the ducts of the glands or pores of the skin. These accumulated materials decay, and the attempts of the skin to carry off this decay produce small pimples or pustules, often preceded by blackheads. Sometimes there is a relation between the child's diet and the severity of the acne, and then regulation of the diet will be of considerable help. The well-known sweet tooth of the teen-ager, which induces him to go on sprees at the soda fountain, may aggravate the condition. Most simple acnes of early adolescence clear up spontaneously when the skin is adjusted to the new activity.

While it lasts, however, it is one of the most troublesome and disturbing problems that the youngster has to meet. At this age, he is particularly prone to deep self-concern and -absorption. His body is new and difficult to handle in every respect. Unsightly blemishes on it will invariably make him miserable. He has a need for perfection which is completely denied by any disfigurement. It is not enough to reassure him about the probably temporary nature of his affliction or to fob him off with the false assertion that it doesn't matter. He should have help in trying to control the condition. If simple dietary or hygienic measures don't do the trick, no time should be lost in consulting a doctor. Many young adolescents have shut themselves away from their associates in their anguish over a severe case of acne. If the condition is very bad, it may persist into adult life or cause permanent scarring.

The author remembers seeing a man of thirty who had suffered from a particularly disfiguring acne during his adolescence. Withdrawing almost entirely from social contacts, he had become a solitary, almost a hermit, with an absolute fixation on his skin. In time, his fixation assumed such proportions that it dictated all the activities of his life. Needless to say, his judgment of his condition was distorted, and his emotional reaction to it had actually produced some of the physical disturbance. This is not an exaggerated case, but just one of the possible results of the misery caused by the child's knowledge of his own disfigurement.

A voice change takes place in both sexes, but it is so much less noticeable in the girl that we act as if it didn't occur at all. The boy, however, undergoes sharp change in the quality and pitch of his voice. It is caused by a thickening of the vocal chords under the influence of the internal secretory glands. A delay in voice change is sometimes embarrassing to a big boy, who is apt to feel the incongruity keenly—to be as large as a man with a voice like a girl's. However, there is nothing that will interfere with the eventual accomplishment of the change short of very severe disorders of sexual development. And in that case the absence of voice change will be only a minor symptom.

All these developments are simply symptoms of much more fundamental and profound changes centering around the achievement of sexual maturity. All of them, internal and external, derive from that principal undertaking and serve its purposes remotely or directly. In the girl they occur considerably earlier than in the boy (she is usually one year or more ahead of her male contemporary). The first noticeable change is the early development of the breasts, followed not much later by the appearance of body hair in its characteristic distribution. These changes precede the beginning of active menstrual life by a period of time varying from six months to two years. Often a girl shows complete breast development before she experiences her first menstrual period. In the boy, the external changes—the beginning of the growth of body hair and the gradual increase in the size of the genitals—seem of greater importance because of their greater obviousness; the girl's development is more internalized.

These developments are effected by the newly activated sexual glands, which, though present from the beginning, are dormant up to this time. The process which sets them off is a complex one dependent upon a chain of events involving all the internal glands. These are so called because they do not have any duct or passageway leading from the gland itself to the outside of the body; instead they deliver their secretions directly into the blood stream, which in turn distributes them throughout the body, to have their effect upon other glands and upon all organs of the body. The secretions of these glands are known as hormones.

The internal secretory system is composed principally of the following glands: the pituitary gland, situated at the base of the brain; the thyroid gland, located at the base of the neck; the parathyroids, behind and at the side of the thyroid; the suprarenal glands, lying over and above the kidneys; the pancreas, slightly to the left and at the back of the abdominal cavity, lying against the spine; and finally the gonads or sex glands.

The sex glands have a double function. They produce important hormones in addition to the reproductive cells, the egg of the female and the sperm cell of the male. The pituitary has two parts. The forward part is the master gland of the entire system. It is this gland that activates the sex glands, brings them harmoniously into the glandular circuit and initiates the process of sexual maturing. The circumstance which touches off this process is not defined, but because of its intimate connections with the central nervous system, it is easy to believe that the switch is thrown ultimately by an emotional factor—the "need to grow up." The same gland also controls growth and determines height and size and keeps these within healthy limits. When its action is interfered with very markedly, one finds giantism or dwarfism or other disturbances in body shape, such as feminine form in the boy and masculine form in the girl. The other part of the pituitary gland produces hormones which regulate the contraction of blood vessels, the muscles of the intestines, uterus and, in fact, all muscles over which we do not have voluntary control. Another fraction of the gland determines the water balance in the body tissues.

The thyroid gland controls the metabolic rate—that is, the rapidity with which oxygen is consumed in the body. A relatively inactive thyroid produces a low metabolic rate, which in turn results in sluggishness, fat, and mental retardation; an overactive thyroid and a consequent high metabolic rate produce a restless, thin, nervous individual with rapid pulse, excessive perspiration, weakness, tremor, exaggerated appetite and intolerance to cold. In addition to its effects on metabolism, the thyroid influences the menstrual cycle, and a deficient thyroid may cause underdevelopment of the genitals. Like other glands, it has a close interaction with the pituitary.

Like the pituitary, the paired adrenal glands have two parts, the inner or medulla, and the outer or cortex, each secreting different products. This gland was described by Dr. George Cannon as the one which prepares the body for "fight or flight." The inner part produces adrenaline, a very important hormone which sets off all those activities which prepare the body to meet an emergency. When it is released into the blood stream, blood pressure rises, the pulse and breathing rate increase, vision becomes more acute, the blood supply to the legs and arms is redistributed, the hair stands on end and the general muscular tension of the body increases. At the same time, any body activity that would interfere with or hinder the individual's capacity to fight or run away is inhibited. Digestion slows down, processes of elimination are halted, and sexual and hunger needs are forgotten. Fright or anger have a similar effect, and at times we can feel these changes taking place within us. The rest of the adrenal, the outer part, is equally vital to life. Disturbances in the cortex caused by disease may end in death or in the wasting illness known as Addison's disease. The cortex also plays an important role in sex development, and tumors here are associated with extraordinary abnormalities of sexual maturing and sex characteristics. New discoveries about the cortex are now in the process of being tested.

The sexual glands—the ovary of the female, the testes of the male—are, of course, most directly concerned in sexual growth, and on their adequate development the ability to reproduce one's kind finally depends. They have a double function and can be considered both internal and external secretory glands. The external secretion of each is its own ultimate product, for the ovary the mature egg and for the testes the mature spermatozoon. In this aspect of their function these two glands are of a particular sort, unrelated to the other internal glands of the body. They carry the reproductive power and all the hereditary and family physical characteristics of past generations. This means that in every mature ovum there is contained the sum total of the hereditary characteristics of that female and in every mature spermatozoon the hereditary characteristics of that male. It is not necessary to go into the complex biological mechanisms that this fact encompasses nor to argue the questions of heredity here. But it is this fact that makes the reproductive glands the center of concern in the developing individual. The drive for the preservation of the species is a drive of such potency and overwhelming force that it pushes toward its goal at all costs. This power of the organism will develop at the expense of any and all other powers and without regard for or connection with those other powers. There is a kind of blind persistence in it which displays no concern for the fitness of the individual; it can appear in full intensity in the most crippled, blunted and degenerate person as well as in the most thoroughly perfected of the race. The maturation of these glands is signalized by the onset of menstruation in the girl and the seminal emission (sometimes called a nocturnal emission because it takes place at night as a "wet dream") in the boy.

It is a mistake to believe that these particular events always indicate the absolute readiness of the youngster for reproduction. They merely usher in the process which, when complete, will provide such readiness. There is a good deal of evidence that the reproductive process is inhibited for varying periods of time after puberty has been reached. This is a peculiarly interesting circumstance, even seemingly contradictory. For if the onset of menstruation and the seminal emission indicate the presence of mature reproductive cells, why should the process be retarded? To be sure, it is not always. But conception immediately or soon after the establishment of puberty is the exception rather than the rule. More is required than simply the mature cells. The fertilized cell must be carried in a mature uterus and the uterus in a mature body, and these are not completed for some time after the child appears to be sexually developed. It is the action of the internal secretion, the hormones of the sex glands, that results finally in a mature individual with all the fully developed attributes, internal and external, that make pregnancy possible.

The function of the ovary is affected by the regulatory powers of the other internal glands. The ovary, in turn, regulates the menstrual cycle, secreting a hormone (estrogen) which produces the menses, thus insuring the complete renovation of the lining of the uterus when no fertilized egg has been received. Following the menses the ovary secretes another hormone which prepares the internal membrane of the uterus for the reception of a fertilized egg so that pregnancy can proceed.

In the case of the male the situation is similar. The mere presence of mature spermatozoa does not necessarily mean that the individual is completely ready for reproduction. There must be other secretory activity to complete the state of readiness and to make the union of the two cells possible. The mature cell is manufactured in the testis but there is needed the secretion of an auxiliary gland, the prostate, to make up the seminal secretion. The prostate lies around the neck of the bladder, and its secretion is delivered into the urethra where it is united with spermatozoa to form the principal components of the fertilizing fluid.

The function of the testis is not confined to the production of male sperm cells. The sperm is the product that is delivered to the outside, but the gland has important internal secretory activities as well. The hormones of the testis are androgens (man-making) and have a very decisive part in insuring the development of a mature male. Body configuration and such characteristic male features as hair and fat distribution as well as voice change are regulated by the male hormones. Without them there is no male.

Finally, it should be realized that sex hormones not only are responsible for all the changes listed above but also exert an enormous influence upon both conscious and unconscious emotions, attitudes and needs, affecting all those more or less intangible qualities which we have in mind when we speak of masculinity and femininity—those qualities that are so difficult to define accurately and that are sensed rather than perceived directly.

With the final maturation of the reproductive apparatus,

physical growth is complete and the individual is prepared for the ultimate physical stresses of adult life. The infinite complexity and the delicate interrelations of sexual maturity with body development can barely be suggested in so brief a presentation. There is a timing and an interaction that are unsurpassable in their accuracy. In the healthy individual, the growth of the body structure itself, the increase in weight and substance, goes along in perfect harmony with the particular and separate organic and glandular developments, to insure, at the time of total growth, a state of complete integration that will serve the body's ultimate purpose of reproduction.

II

Emotional and Intellectual Development

As there is a physical adult, so there is an emotional adult. When we define in a general way what it requires to be an adult emotionally, we will see more clearly how far from emotional maturity the child is before adolescence. The formidable nature of the task that confronts him will then be apparent.

If we were to name the salient marks of a mature emotional development, we would list the acceptance of responsibility as a counterpoise to privilege; the capacity for giving and receiving love; the ability to tolerate a delay in getting satisfaction. These qualities have a wide expression in life.

The grown-up individual is competent and independent. This self-reliance applies to his inner and outer problems. He will know how to care for himself materially and physically. Moreover, his sense of responsibility will extend to others besides himself. If he has a family, he will not be negligent or resentful of the fact that he is accountable for their care and welfare. He won't expect that he can get something for nothing. He will know that work is the order of the day and that he can't expect to be dependent on others. He will enjoy his right to make his own choices and his own decisions but he will know that he gets what he earns, in the large sense.

Really grown-up people do not have to act on every impulse. They can wait for their satisfactions and give up the immediate and lesser for the future and greater. They are not at the mercy of every pressure they feel. They have a certain mastery over their emotional expressions. *He* won't become the terror of the home if his every demand isn't catered to, nor will *she* have a tantrum whenever the budget won't cover a momentary desire.

Adults, if they are entitled to be called so, know pretty well who they are, what they believe in and what they want to do and be. They will have arrived at a working arrangement of values by which they regulate their lives. The adult doesn't mourn today and forget tomorrow; he doesn't sway from one loyalty to another; he doesn't get drunk because he has run into a spot of trouble; he doesn't leave home when things are dull; he doesn't quit his job the first time anyone questions him. Adults show steadiness in their love relations. They are able to make choices and stand by them. They can show control over their sexual lives and be responsible for their sexual behavior. They expect and want children as part of their lives and loving. They can give love without having to get an immediate return. They can stand a certain amount of disappointment and frustration and still be able to function. Without these powers parenthood would be a thankless drudgery and real citizenship an impossibility.

No one for a moment imagines that the youngster, upon arriving at puberty, can measure up to these requirements. The development of these qualities is precisely the task life now sets him. It is no trivial assignment, and there are too many who cannot accomplish it and so live all their lives as adolescents. But the very need to do and be these things and have the satisfactions they bring determines the problem. All the strength the youngster has been able to acquire, all the increased strength he will develop as his growth proceeds, will be mobilized to this end. These new and steadily more pressing demands are more and more insistently felt. They force the issue, making the youngster struggle to grow in order to be able to satisfy them. To do it requires revolutionary changes. The dynamo which provides the power is the sexual drive. The child has always been a sexual individual but previously he has felt only a blind indiscriminate push toward pleasure from any source, any person, in any way. Now all that is changed. Now the drive is surely and inescapably sexual, and the youngster knows it and knows something of its meaning. It is related to clear body demands. It establishes its direction and its purpose without any doubt or question. That purpose is sexual satisfaction involving the reproductive apparatus. Right here the problem is posed.

That it is a difficult one for the child to solve is now a well-understood fact. Many factors operating both within and without the growing boy or girl make that inevitable. There are barriers to easy expression and direct satisfactions. If the child lived in some simpler, more primitive society he would find things simpler. When puberty began he might be taken away from his mother's house and initiated into the privileges of manhood. Once this was done, he would be expected to marry. But no such easy path is laid out for modern youngsters in Western society. They will not be expected or allowed to get seriously involved with each other until much later, when they are also equipped educationally, socially and economically. Furthermore, they are not given any other outlet for sexual expression. There is an understanding that sexual expression is not allowed to those who are not married. Never mind that often this restriction is apparently too flabby to have much effect. There is still strength in it and there is punishment for those who break it. It is stringent enough to make the breaking hard and hedged around with guilt. So the adolescent is faced with a life in which there is a decided lag between the time when he is ready to use his sexual power and the time when society is ready to let him do so.

There are not only the external regulations to deal with but those which operate within the boy and girl themselves. These are no less restrictive or difficult to cope with than those imposed by society. In the first place, the child entering his teens is in strange territory without any landmarks. He is quite simply afraid of the newness and the unknown dangers. Every new experience encountered in the course of growing up arouses some apprehension, and such a tremendous undertaking as this, particularly, is approached with uncertainty at first. Nevertheless, for most youngsters, this is a time of excitement and pleasure, and anticipation of long-promised and awaited satisfactions. Some children on the other hand show obvious signs of resenting and fearing the beginning of their sexual lives.

One youngster I know was so rebellious about it all that she turned her back on it, as it were. She tried to ignore the facts. She refused to wear girl's clothes and insisted upon having her hair cut like her brother's. If an occasion requiring girl's dress arose, she simply sidestepped it, refusing flatly to participate. She lived in blue jeans and boy's shirts. Anything that was said or done to induce her to do otherwise was a signal for a temper outburst. She was outspoken in her determination to ignore the whole business. She had never wanted to grow up at all and certainly, if it had to be, she was going to be a boy and not a girl. Soon she was in a predicament. The boys would no longer let her take part in their games and the girls were contemptuous of her. For her, two things were true. Her mother had always given her attention and love to the younger babies in the family, especially to her brother, who was much the favorite. The argument was simple: if you want mother's love, you will have to stay a baby and preferably a boy baby. Of course, the situation is only rarely as obvious and extreme as this. Most youngsters welcome, even if with some apprehension, the thought of growing up, sometimes to the point of trying to anticipate its privileges.

The unconscious elements of the emotional life further compound the difficulty of the child's task. The child's first love is necessarily his parents, since they make up his first world and provide his first security. At some point in the course of the early years (from four to seven) he selects the parent of the opposite sex as the object of his love and the source from which he hopes to get satisfaction. This situation was labeled by Freud the "Oedipus complex," from the name of the Greek king who murdered his father and married his mother. The consequences of these feelings are unpleasant to the child and provoke a great deal of anxiety. For, wanting the parent of the opposite sex for himself, he is inevitably hostile to and resentful of the parent of his own sex, who stands in the way of his having what he wants. His hostility arouses in him a sense of guilt and anxiety; and because of this, and also in exchange for the love of his parents, he makes a great effort to give up the forbidden and dangerous wishes. The way in which he solves this problem is of first importance to his later development. If he is successful in giving up his guilty desires and freeing himself of his resentment, all is likely to be well. But at this early point in his development no more is asked of the young child than that he put the whole question aside for future settlement.

That future settlement has to be made "for keeps" during adolescence. At that time there begins a struggle between his love for his parents and his wish to be entirely free to grow up. Here the adolescent finds himself in a tough position from which for the moment there seems to be little way out. Every path is blocked, and only when he has mastered the inner difficulties and outgrown the external ones, is the way open to full expression. Reality is in favor of the good solution, and the happy fact is that most people manage it, even if there are some flaws in the final settlement.

It is certain the youngster cannot find any real satisfaction in clinging to his parents. The drive of the inner need for ultimate gratification keeps the child always pushing toward more adult ways of feeling. He cannot simply give up the impulse to full maturity and return to being a child. This would be to choose a kind of death. Parents must be relinquished as sources of satisfactions, and new sources must be found. This is not an easy assignment. If he gives up his attachment to his parents—so the child fears—they may no longer be so willing to protect and cherish him; indeed, he may sacrifice the very thing on which he has always leaned for all the necessities and satisfactions of his life. To give up dependence and its comfortable passivity is to relinquish one of the earliest and most cherished of all the privileges of childhood. But the pressure of growth, the urgency of development, call upon every resource the youngster has been able to acquire to carry out the task. The picture of adolescence is formed by the action and interaction of the forces directed to the accomplishment of this end.

The deepest drive of the whole undertaking is to develop emotional freedom from the parents. That this is not easy the existence of so many adults who have never achieved it testifies. It takes a great deal of energy and it is tackled with corresponding intensity and violence. The effort will not always be consistent nor the course steady; there will be an enormous amount of zigzagging and twisting. At times the child will be exaggeratedly assertive; at others just the opposite. What underlies this seeming purposelessness is clear. The child is driven to his task of changing his relations with his parents, depriving them of their old meaning and freeing himself for new attachments. But the hold on him of the old and the secure is very strong and his fear of the new and possibly dangerous is at times just as strong. To master both these feelings, to strive toward maturity despite them, calls for a big effort, and in making it the youngster mobilizes every bit of energy at his command. The effect, inevitably, is one of exaggerated intensity and force.

Also inevitably, there will be periods of failure, of back-sliding, when to the parent the youngster will seem to be his "old adorable self." But it is exactly his old self that he must not be. He has a strict mandate to be a new and unique self. In the course of his metamorphosis he may at times be extremely defiant and appear almost to deny his parents and their influence. Up to this time his attachment to them has impelled him to learn to feel as they feel, to be as they are. Earlier, when he was wrestling with the problem of his hostility toward the parent of the same sex because of his wish for the parent of the opposite sex, he ultimately made his solution through giving up the hostility and substituting identification. Thus he said, as it were, "I am like mother (father). I do not hate her (him). I love her (him) and wish to be as she (he) is. I shall have the same gratifications that she (he) has when I come of age." Now, however, this is not enough. He has a larger assignment than that. Because he must be himself and himself alone, he may modify this identity with the parent in order to be sure of his own individuality. He may identify himself violently with every sort of antiparental ideal imaginable—this is the time of wild enthusiasms and frantic denials. Or he may become actively hostile. One does not love the person whom one emphatically dislikes. Q.E.D. But soon, chameleon-like, the old child will reappear, all compliance and love.

The changes of this age, as bewildering to the youngster as to those around him, appear to be entirely senseless, irrational, without pattern, and we may wonder why the process of growing up cannot proceed to its appointed conclusion smoothly and without so much turmoil. The answer is in the intrinsic meaning of adolescence itself. All its implications are in direct opposition to the established and long-held devotions of the child's life. He is giving up cherished convictions. He is moving toward the very desire that has been so long forbidden. He is entering a relationship that will make demands for responsible behavior and that he will have to engage in without help. He is asserting his independence. He may be sacrificing the love and devotion of his parents. What more natural, under the circumstances, than that he should be hesitant, vacillatory, indecisive? Childhood may never look so desirable as at that moment when adult life beckons most strongly. All this is part of the everyday family situation if it is not exaggerated to the size of a real problem. Usually, parents are able to take it in their stride and get a good deal of pleasure out of seeing and participating in so exciting a process. The swings of attitude and mood, in any case, grow less stormy and extreme as the youngster begins to gain a sense of mastery over himself.

Parents have a decisive role to play in support of the child. They still provide the most important part of the environment, and the environment greatly affects the process of maturing. What is needed is understanding and acceptance along with strength. If the parent is frightened or resentful of the whole process, the youngster has an added burden. He will need to be even more vigorously determined to go ahead with his growing up, or he will have to give up. Sometimes this may lead him to overreach himself, and in struggling to free himself from the restraining parents, come to grief. For such a young person, the loss of his parents' regard is less of a threat than the peril in clinging to the old patterns and old attachments. The same kind of thing can happen if parents who have become dependent on the child's love feel threatened with its loss. Such parents will never recognize their own culpability; rather they will find a thousand reasons why their wish to keep the child in leading strings is in reality only a rightful desire to protect and safeguard him.

One woman of this type was bewildered and hurt when faced with the violent reaction of her daughter. She complained that the child was entirely uncontrollable, couldn't be relied upon, was associating with improper people, was in great danger of running into sexual difficulties and altogether was "going to be the death of me." All her life the girl had been the object of her mother's wish for accomplishment and conformity. The mother lavished attention on her and dictated her every move. Unhappily married, she was intensely dependent on her daughter, and sought in her recompense for the lack of her husband's love. She had so hoped that "we would be companions." She wanted, as far as possible, to retard the growth process and keep her daughter with herself. The girl dimly saw all this and complained bitterly that her mother would never let her "be herself" or do anything except what the mother herself wanted or approved of or had done. She deeply wanted her mother's sympathy, but saw no way of getting it except by giving in to her every whim. She chose the other path of stubborn, sullen defiance, couldn't endure anything her mother allied herself with, and detested her mother's friends and associates as well as her interests and standards. She was going to be herself if it cost her everything she had of security and love.

Not much better are those parents who are anxious to do nothing that might interfere with the youngster's "freedom." This attitude can be a thin disguise for a kind of abandonment, which leaves the boy or girl to his own unaided strength. His own strength isn't enough in the strenuous times he has to face. The child has always needed power to lean on and the need persists at this age. The very little child has no real strength of his own. He must "borrow," and the lender is the parent. The parents' belief in him, their willingness to regulate and provide for him are all sources of this borrowed strength. So fortified, he is enabled to protect himself not only from outside difficulties but from the inner forces that threaten to overpower him.

To a remarkable degree, the years of adolescence repeat on a grand scale the years of infancy. The stake this time is the individual's adult life and his later happiness. It must all be settled now and settled finally. This is his "last chance." The attachment to parents must be dissolved and the ability to find outside love must be acquired or all the rest of life will be crippled and incomplete. But because the forces holding the child to the old pattern as well as those pushing him into new and dangerous activity are at times more than he can contend with, parental strength is vital to the enterprise. Steady support to the youngster's attempt to find independence or the steady restraint of those who would overextend themselves is invaluable.

But they aren't forthcoming from parents who abdicate their position as soon as the youngster is in his teens. The adolescent in such circumstances may come to grief through his own weakness and helplessness. The parents who stand ready to be firm and strong—a balance to the youngster's intensity and inconsistency—are the parents who answer the child's needs. They will not expect strength where it cannot yet exist. They will supply what is lacking in the child's own equipment. They will lend strength where it is needed. They will neither push nor hold back the growth process arbitrarily. They will try to gauge the real strength of their youngsters and give the appropriate help or withhold it. They will not be carried away by the child's uncontrolled swings of mood, interest or behavior. There will be no wish to cling to the youngster as a source of love satisfaction, nor any wish to escape giving him the real love which is support and understanding. In such a climate the youngster's powers grow more easily and comfortably. The struggle goes on; inner strength increases; the true sexual constitution is firmly established. Less and less often will the youngster need to touch home base, or strengthen himself by drawing on the strength of his parents.

During the time of adolescence sexual impulse is pushing against both inner barriers and outer regulations. The inner barriers are those erected against the old ways, the old loves —the taboo against incest. They say, *"Not* this way! Direct your search elsewhere, toward new objects." But when that is done, the outer regulations are encountered, the restrictions of society, which also has a stake in all this. These, in turn, say, "Not yet. Wait until you are older." These prohibitions force upon the youngster some compromise. One of the forms of compromise is masturbation. This is a word which has had horrendous connotations for almost as long as it has had any known meaning. The Bible provided specific sanctions against it; supposed "scientific" learning found it to be unequivocally harmful; folklore and custom argued that it was sure to be noxious in its results. It was (and often still is) held responsible for every imaginable horror. Variously, insanity, impotence, sterility, criminality, acne, blindness, rings under the eyes, or lameness have been ascribed to it. It causes none of these things. So far as medical science now knows, the one noxious result of masturbation is guilt and the mental torment that goes with it. That, in turn, is the result not of the indulgence itself but of the attitudes toward it.

The facts are that masturbation is of practically universal occurrence during two periods of life. The first is during infancy, from about four to seven. This period coincides with the emergence of the first conflict over sex—the Oedipus complex, with its drive toward the parent of the opposite sex. When this drive is frustrated, as it usually is, the child in his disappointment turns to himself. He finds that he is able to get satisfaction from his own body. Masturbation thus becomes a substitute for and an equivalent of the guilty wishes directed toward his parents. This fact supplies its intolerable quality. If masturbation equals incest, it cannot be anything but taboo. The parent almost unfailingly re-enforces its guilty quality by opposing it and punishing the child.

Masturbation in adolescence represents a return of these same drives and compromises. Now, however, what was hidden is open, what was vague is clear, what unconscious, conscious. Guilt is therefore greater and more agonizing than before and must be met head on. The youngster very often is caught in a trap of alternating guilt and renunciation. One day's vow is followed by the next day's fall from grace. All of this is something about which the young person is almost always unyieldingly secretive. Occasionally, an uninformed boy or girl believes that he or she has come upon a peculiar, unique vice never before practiced. He feels set apart in his shame and disgrace—a pariah. It is close to impossible to appreciate the anguish suffered by the youngster in such a predicament. Precisely because of its intensely painful quality, most adults (most parents) have long since pushed it out of their consciousness and relegated it to the category of forgotten shame.

Parents frequently ask: How can I tell whether my boy or girl is having these troubles? How can I tell if he is masturbating at all? What can I do to help him? Shall I talk to him about it or shall I send him to someone to be instructed? Or shall I ignore it? All these practical questions we shall try to answer in the following sections where the details of the behavior problems associated with adolescence will be dealt with. For the time being we are concerning ourselves with its meaning. Actually, masturbation is part of man's *Via Sacra* to adult living, and a nearly inevitable part of his growing up. It has its purpose. It solves a problem, or part of one, for a while. It postpones the necessity to cope with the ultimate, for it is beyond the power of the youngster to proceed at once to a full sexual expression. It is impossible to go backward, to retreat to the forbidden parental love relation. Compromise and appeasement, worrying as they may be, are then the only solutions that the psyche has to offer. Beyond this there is a positive purpose. The pathways are kept defined. The supremacy of the genital as the source of final pleasure is reaffirmed and maintained.

This phase of adolescence begins and ends at various times in various children, nor does it have any sharp beginning and ending. It may overlap other more or less "advanced" stages. The happy fact, however, is that in most youngsters the drive toward maturity is ultimately strong enough to master the more infantile tendency to self-love. In the adult, under the usual circumstances this tendency has disappeared entirely.

At some point, usually fairly early in adolescence, we are apt to encounter a special method of dealing with the sexual problems it presents. During this phase, which we can call the homosexual phase, the youngster appears to put by the problem of coping with his relations with the opposite sex and to turn his attention and love toward someone of his own sex. This he will do with greater or lesser obviousness and intensity for a longer or shorter period of time. It may be entirely conscious or it may be largely unconscious. When it is unconscious, it consists only of a kind of delicate tenderness between the two people. There will be an entire absence of any awareness of the quality of the relationship. All the recognizable sexual elements will have been successfully placed in the unconscious. In other circumstances, the feelings will be less unconscious and the sexual aspect of the relationship will be entirely evident to the two youngsters themselves. The exchanges between them may be of the most explicit sexual nature.

Sometimes the object of this feeling is another youngster. Then there may be a Damon and Pythias relationship characterized by the most exquisite feelings of loyalty and closeness. The two may become as one, sharing every thought and feeling, inseparable, complete together, imperfect when separate. At other times, a youngster may develop such feelings for an adult other than his mother or father. This is hero worship. The loved one is at once the ideal image of the child and himself. Adoration is the best word to describe the state of mind in which the child finds himself. He will wish to pattern himself on the loved parent substitute, to live up to the ideals he associates with him, to become his devoted slave. At its less intense level, there is a great fealty, great fondness and admiration. There is purpose in all this. Such a relationship acts as a sluiceway, a safety valve for all the unmanageable feelings with which the young person may be beset. Love his parent he may not. Love himself he must not. But to love another, a different parent, another, often a better self, may offer a compromise, a way out.

If we understand all this, there is little to disturb us, little we must oppose. The inner requirements are being met, the problems being solved somehow. There may be times when these situations will last longer than they should. There will be some youngsters for whom this experience is only the beginning of a prolonged difficulty. For some few, it will be the beginning of a situation that will never change. Of these we shall speak especially, so we need here concern ourselves only with the common experience. Usually the period is self-limited and lasts a relatively short time, giving way before the steady push to achieve real adult satisfactions.

The problem of the parents during these years is particularly vexing, because it requires that they understand themselves as well as their youngsters. Parenthood means in

some measure reliving life with the child. Through a kind
of identity with him, parents re-encounter themselves. In
doing so, they meet their old problems in whatever state
of solution they were buried, hopefully to be forgotten.
It is axiomatic that we all, as parents, resent and oppose
those things in our children which real self-knowledge and
honesty would make us admit we were most ashamed of in
ourselves. The ancient accusation, "You're just like your
father or mother," really means, "You're just like the objec-
tionable part of myself." Generally this feeling is unconscious, to be sure, but it is even more powerful because of
that. All grown-ups, obviously, are closer to their adolescence
than to any other part of their past; and some always re-
tain many adolescent attitudes. Take for example the problem of masturbation. To face it in the child may force the
parents to face it unconsciously in themselves. This can
easily rekindle their own repressed guilt, which in turn
may lead them to adopt a severely punishing attitude
toward the child. In effect, they are punishing themselves
through punishing the youngster.

Gradually the issue of the developmental struggle is seen
to be clearly in favor of maturity. More and more the
young person shows an adult attitude. It is not a quick
process, nor—again it must be emphasized—an orderly
one, but characterized by much indecision, vacillation and
confusion. But by the use of all the devices we have discussed—new ideals, new objects toward whom to direct
love, repeated testing in reality—the youngster comes
closer to his goal. A boy or girl of fourteen is all chaos and
disorder. The same youngster by the time he is twenty has
gone very far toward a poised and directed maturity. Fourteen does not know what he wants, whether he will be
surely man or woman, what life interests he will devote himself to. He still wants to lean heavily on his parents and is
often pure child. Twenty is sure of himself, is now de-

cisively a boy or girl, has determined his major interests, is less and less dependent on his parents and has almost conclusively turned his back on his childhood attitudes. The "almost" allows for considerable margin. In many respects twenty is still reminiscent of much earlier years. But essentially the conclusion should be near at hand—boy to be independent man—girl to be independent woman. Once the choice is effectively made, the issues are clearer and the effort more closely directed to the final solution of finding a partner who will satisfy all requirements.

It is this which gives the characteristic pattern to the last period of adolescence. The young person is consumed with the need to win the approval of the opposite sex, to meet and know many boys or girls, so that choice may be wide and inclusive. The impulse to give expression to the sexual longing becomes very insistent. Choices are made and relinquished, often with bewildering speed, though each, of course, seemed final at the moment. This is the time too when the sexual impulse leads most frequently to direct sexual experience, and when the consequences in misery and confusion are most commonly seen. Occasionally, even now, the youngster will briefly show signs of wishing to revert to his earlier, more carefree and less exacting years. The intensity, the variability are still evident, but the tendency is toward a leveling off.

There is pressure toward full sexual expression and there is pressure against it at the same time. These counterpressures come from both inner and outer sources. Part of the environment gives permission; part withholds it. So with the youngster's own attitudes. There is inner hesitation as well as inner compulsion. Presumably at the time that the inner and outer forces come into balance and active sexual life begins, we should be able to say that adult life has begun. Ideally this would be so, and in the ideal adolescent (whoever and wherever he may be) it is so. For at the time

when all the contrary drives within the youngster are har-
monized, he will have mastered himself and have formed
a life that will permit him to assume the responsibilities
that are compatible with marriage. At this point, his task
is presumed to be completed and he is entering the early
stages of adult life.

III

Social Changes of Adolescence

Adolescence propels the young person into a new and constantly widening relationship with his environment. Here he finds an arena for testing new attitudes, ideals and ideas. Until now his social life has been focused on the family rather than on the wider community. Safety has required that he stay close to his parents and learn to handle himself inside the small community in order to gain the strength and skill to handle the problems of the larger society. Home and school are the two areas with which he is familiar. In school he is in a group of youngsters of his own age, whose capacities are closely equal to his own. He is under the supervision of a teacher who knows what can be expected and will not make demands which are beyond his capacities. At home he has had similar consideration. Beyond these relatively narrow confines, experience is incomplete and knowledge inadequate.

The time between babyhood and puberty seems especially designed to give the developing child a chance to prepare himself for the effort that adolescence will demand of him. He learns what the real world around him is like. Added knowledge brings added power, and the ability to tackle more difficult situations. No one is able to meet and cope with situations he does not understand. So with the child. He does not know what will hurt him and what will benefit him unless he is taught. All his baby days he is learning by experience and by encouragement and warning. "Let's

31

go into the water! Isn't the dog nice—pet him. Careful, it's hot! Um, it's good. Watch for the step. I wouldn't eat that stick if I were you. Running with scissors in your hands is probably a bad idea. It's all right, it's just a tiny cut. Oops, get up, it didn't really hurt. A 'Band-Aid' will fix it."

The life of a youngster, as soon as he is able to move, becomes a network of these assurances, cautions and trials. School begins to formalize and extend it. The tools of learning are secured and mastery is extended in ever increasing ways. Knowledge and understanding of the environment outside of the home broaden. Little by little the restrictions become fewer and his interests and powers widen. He can go to the corner on an errand; he can get to and from school alone; he can find his way safely to a friend's house. In short, growing independence sends him farther and farther afield on his own.

The advancement is continuous. More power is acquired all the time. More responsibility can be tolerated in more ways about more things. There is more self-assurance. In much that he does, the child foreshadows his later development. His ever widening intellectual interests, for example, give a clear indication of his later social concerns. These changes do not take place abruptly but with a gradualness which is at times scarcely perceptible, so natural and inevitable do they appear. Nevertheless, before puberty, the child is in most things still a child and as yet some way from being able to cope with the demands of adolescence.

When the teens are reached, his horizons widen considerably, and he feels a compulsion to try his strength in a bigger arena. As a result he comes in contact with the larger community and all its agencies, institutions and forces as he has not before. Now he is beginning to show a constantly expanding concern with the social organization of which he is becoming an independent part. There is an enormous widening in his range of interests, and his intellectual life begins to assume the quality of an adult's. School reflects this. Having acquired the fundamental tools, he can actually start to get an education. He can begin to do independent thinking as well as increase his stock of knowledge. The nature of his thinking changes in the direction of deepened understanding in the field of abstract ideas.

This new development is vital to the making of judgments and the establishment of ideals and standards. It is a grown-up talent. This is obvious to anyone who compares the way in which a child of fourteen looks at moral problems with the way a child of ten does. The ten-year-old has acquired a handy set of regulations. Take the notion of sportsmanship and consideration of others. Children of ten have a strict sense of playground fairness and justice which includes such notions as "Don't hit a fellow when he is down"—"Don't pick on anybody smaller than yourself"—"Don't cheat in games." The child of fourteen still has these rules but is beginning to integrate them with a wider concept which takes in over-all ideals of justice and fairness. The child of ten is still operating on the premise that he is likely to get into trouble himself unless he follows the rules. The child of fourteen may be beginning to feel the need for a moral ideal which will be in conformity with his own nature and not simply a practical way of keeping out of trouble. When he arrives at this point, justice is no longer a matter of playground convenience but is becoming a profound conviction.

As things acquire long-term significance, and as meanings broaden and deepen, the child inevitably begins to reappraise the society in which he lives and to form identifications outside his family, the school, or his own small gang. Now he must find his place in the world and to do this he must experiment. His investigations may lead him to associate himself with one social group after another and to adopt their attitudes. At first the attachments will not last long but they are nevertheless important; they are his way of "finding out." Parents may be astonished by the widely roving concerns of children who only the day before yesterday were interested in the next baseball game and how to get out of washing their necks.

Everything now is grist to the mill. Anything can capture the imagination and devotion of the youngster. All intellectual activity is opened to him—artistic, social, political, philosophical, economic. He will try to judge all situations by his new attitudes and standards. The social and political scene, for example, may be particularly interesting and challenging. It is well suited to his emerging preoccupations with judgments and values. In his approach, his new idealism is intense and often rigid and uncompromising. The notions of justice and injustice, loyalty and treachery, devotion and inconstancy, love and hate, fair play and dishonesty all stand out in violent contrast and with great force. Everything is seen to be in unyielding opposition to something else. This is the time of absolute right and absolute wrong. Compromise is abhorrent. There will be complete intolerance for anything that violates the ideals and principles to which the child is now committed. When disillusioned or disappointed in a particular object of devotion, he will cast it aside for another that seems to provide the perfection which he is seeking. Youngsters at this age develop blind and fanatical attachment to causes and isms of all sorts, sometimes going from one to another with startling rapidity. Provided only that a notion holds out the hope of the millenium, they are easily won adherents. Very often their attachments and partisan attitudes are radically different from the convictions of the family.

A rather conservative but very devoted father found this out when his young son developed a seemingly passionate allegiance to a certain leftist philosophy, and announced it widely. There was thought of hastily removing the errant youngster from the halls of learning which presumably were corrupting him. Wisely, the parents decided to wait, and the young man soon transferred his interest to the religious life. He subsequently went through several further attachments to absolute ideas, finally arriving at a point not far from where his family stood.

Not only as concerns social and political ideas, but in the intellectual sphere, too, these youngsters show the same wide range of interests and often the same tendency to swift change. One day it may be art and the next music, followed soon by poetry, and all three then abandoned for philosophy. They will enjoy a kind of constant prodding, investigation and inspection of every sort of idea that has ever challenged and attracted the minds of men. Furthermore, they can produce an endless amount of talk about it. This is one of the most endearing and distinctive characteristics of adolescent social life. Nothing could be more typical than the tireless discussion, the interminable argument, the "bull session" in which the fate of the world is determined. With it all there is the enthusiasm and intensity that are always to be seen in adolescent life.

Clubs and societies flourish at this age. There are some dangers in this situation and it needs to be watched. Clubs are often extremely excluding and tend to split the community of youngsters into divergent and antagonistic cliques. Their existence can inflict endless pain on those who are not accepted. Where they do not exist, acceptance by their fellows may not be any greater for the individual boy or girl, but nonacceptance, at least, isn't a formalized thing. Clubs may congeal and consolidate associations which would otherwise be more fluid and inclusive. At their worst, they are organizations of unhappy and ill-adjusted young people who are bent on attacking the world they live in— the teen-age deliquent gang. Happily, most adolescent societies are not only far from nefarious in character; they are innocence itself. The fact is that the tendency to form groups has a legitimate and healthy background. The need of young people to be close to each other and to find out, always to find out, as well as to associate with others who have similar likes. It is a tendency that has great strength in adolescence, and it can be put to good use, for it offers endless opportunities to provide the help and guidance which are so sorely needed now. By an appeal to common interests and aspirations, wise parents can promote the formation of groups that not only will give the youngsters much personal satisfaction, but will stimulate their growth in healthy and positive ways.

Anxiety over the possibility that the "club" may degenerate into the "gang" leads many parents to see danger in all close groupings of the young and inexperienced. But the gang is a good thing gone wrong and doesn't invalidate the good thing. The danger lies in the potential attraction and influence that such daring and glamorous groups may have on the less stable and most suggestible children in the community. Some youngsters are so firmly set in a healthy mold that they cannot be influenced in any other direction. Others, less healthy and fortunate, are easily drawn into antisocial groups, which may activate characteristics or tendencies that would otherwise have remained latent and perhaps finally been resolved in a socially useful way.

This was surely the case with a boy of fourteen who had become openly defiant and who associated himself with the most undesirable youngsters in the community, a crowd that was recognized as on the verge of outright delinquency. His parents were frantic, for the boy wasn't susceptible to any approach they made—and small wonder when one knew the underlying situation. They were themselves troubled and unable to provide him with any security. His father was a brilliant but unstable man who kept the family in constant difficulty by his uncontrolled drinking, and often disappeared for days at a time. The boy had none of the things that other boys had. He was so troubled and worried that he did badly in school in spite of a really notable endowment. He was the despair of everyone. The boys whom he admired paid no attention to him because he was not able to participate in their activities and was too unreliable. He was pathetically eager to be accepted by those around him and when the group of near delinquents saw a likely convert in him, he was given an enthusiastic reception to the gang. He was troubled by it and didn't like it, always trying to steer clear of anything dangerous or outright delinquent. But he could not resist the feeling of being loved and accepted that these boys gave him. He was also drawn to their activities, hostile in character, by his own resentments toward his parents. A little help was enough to rescue him from this potentially destructive alliance.

Parents are often uncertain how best to handle this group instinct. The most important thing is to know the nature of the association and the quality of the young people who make up the group. To oppose this tendency is worse than absurd; it is obstructionist, it opposes living activity. To guide and direct it, to control it if it gets out of hand, is the part of intelligence. It is obvious sense to investigate anything with which the young boy or girl associates himself. This can easily be done in a positive way without taking an attitude of opposition. To offer the home as the meeting place is the simplest and most sensible approach. Other parents whose youngsters are also members of the group can be helpful. If parents can learn to pool their experience and their thought, they can do a lot to bring order and sense into their children's lives.

Parents must understand the values to the young person of all of these various adolescent impulses if they are not to be disturbed by them. If they have no recollection of their own salad days, they may try to treat it all as midsummer madness. They ask themselves, "Will my fifteen-year-old really persist in being a vegetarian anarchist who insists upon doing nothing but listen to music all day long?" The chances are against it. Parents may also, after exposure to the long researches into the chosen destiny of the young, have the pardonable notion that before one decides what he is or intends to be, what he will or will not eat, one would be well advised to find out how to get anything to eat at all. They are likely to show little tolerance for the undirected and apparently aimless investigation and thinking that is so much a part of the adolescent mood unless they keep in mind its value as a part of growth.

The parental allegiance to reality has its virtues. It is part of the parents' function, and an important part, to keep a clear view of reality and sometimes to help the young focus squarely on it. The youngster may bemoan his parents' lack of understanding but he will find help and strength in it at the same time. Unless the parents' determination to be "realistic" is only a thin disguise for hostility and rejection, it can be a vital part of the youngster's life. Where there is only antagonism, the boy or girl may be alienated from parental guidance and exposed to the dangers of isolation. Or he may feel a great deal of guilt about his own resentment of the hostile parents, which may make him give up his efforts to achieve his independence.

So to take the attitude that the adolescent is silly and concerned with nebulous nonsense is a dangerous practice. Communication between parents and children will be broken or reduced to nonessentials. The goal is to keep this line intact, to hold the confidence and good feeling of the child. To do this one must take him seriously; his attitudes and feelings must be given reasonable consideration and value. Here, as in all the other vital areas of the adolescent's life, the parent has his opportunity to remain a force and a power. The alternative is to forfeit the respect of the youngster and thereby become useless to him. Parents often bemoan the fact that their child "won't tell me what's on his mind." How can any right-minded or sensible youngster be expected to tell what's on his mind to a parent who either is too bored to listen or belittles and ridicules what the child has to offer?

For the parents there is also a great loss, for they deprive themselves of the pleasure of participating in an exciting adventure. Throughout their children's lives there was always the opportunity—if the parents cared to take it—to relive and re-experience their own past. Now they have a chance to share the brilliance and luminosity of the final unfolding.

However much and however wisely the parent is able to enter into their quest, young people will still need to investigate and explore, discuss and dissect with their contemporaries. After all, they feel the parents must have somehow settled all these questions, long ago—even if badly and mistakenly. Only those who are like oneself, of one's own kind, can really share and really understand. This feeling tends to produce a sense of solidarity, a true communion of friendship which is one of the real things for which the youngster is striving and one of the most valuable products of the exertions he is going through. Sometimes the parents will envy these intimacies and wish to interfere with them. They will believe that they are only seeking their children's confidence. They may insist, "You can tell us everything" and "We would rather you told us than anyone else." This may or may not be true, and the child may or may not believe it. But even if he does, it is his contemporaries with whom he wishes to share. For they are the ones who are having his experiences. His time is different from all other times; he is entering a world of which he knows nothing and under circumstances which were never duplicated. He is separated from his parents by a generation of time and, for him, an eternity of experience. His life is to be lived with his contemporaries and his problems solved in his own time.

Sometimes, a parent's attempt to share everything with his child is dictated by a reluctance to let him grow up, a wish to hold on to him as a source of love and security. This too the child will recognize, resent and turn away from.

As the child grows older, his social life takes a firmer direction. It is now focused definitely on finding a solution to the love and mating problem. At this point the boy-girl situation is ushered in with a vengeance. Because this means that the boy or girl has to some extent settled the fact of his own sexuality, it is gratifying evidence of a maturity which the parent should welcome. The child is now on the last lap of his struggle to maturity. It will not be a straight course. There will be a lot of backing and filling but, by and large, the show is on. The predominating interest in the opposite sex, the need to be chosen, is constantly evident. There are mercurial swings of mood as the enterprise fares well or badly. On the day when the current choice is unresponsive the young person is depressed and gloomy. A friendly nod will send his spirits soaring. Elation and misery succeed each other with kaleidoscopic speed. Choices are changed overnight. It is a time of trial and error. Today's passion is tomorrow's bête noire.

In the beginning the need is general rather than specific. To be "popular," to be "chosen," to have a "date," to get a bid to a dance or a prom, all these are more important than the individuals involved. Reassurance and proof that one is valuable physically is what is needed. No specific choice, no final choice can be made until that is settled. In any case, it would be too difficult and too conclusive at this age to be tied to one individual. That comes later. At first it is enough to be directed in the path leading to heterosexual life.

There is not always a complete acceptance for this program. The door to childhood is not yet closed and this safe haven may still look sweet. But the hard facts again and again force the issue: There cannot be any real or lasting gratification in that choice. So gradually the pace increases and the drive intensifies. The next stage is characterized by an effort to narrow the problem still more; it is the stage of definite choices. This phase will be particularly notable for the seriousness of its attachments. The young people will be anxious to "go steady." Soon after, engagements will be announced. Perhaps there will be several successive engagements. At this point the youngster feels more and more confident and is probably close to what should be a final solution.

Not all young people find themselves in such a happy way. Some may be unusually slow to accept the onrushing events, and others may reject them altogether. The sexual part of life, especially, may be violently rejected by many youngsters, while others may show a very premature determination to plunge into sexual experiences for which they are not ready. Parents are apt to find the precocious youngster a more worrisome problem than the retarded one. The child to whom sexual maturity comes slowly they seem to regard as being in a particularly happy case. But the happiness is more his parents' than his. For what they consider a welcome postponement of trouble is for him an attempt to deal with an unwelcome but inescapable situation. He is just completely afraid of facing the racket. He knows it and he knows that others know it, so he stays entirely away from the arena of struggle. The precocious youngster is also afraid, but he is afraid of different things. He is so afraid that he has a poor grip on his own sexuality and is obliged to prove it early and often. His situation is fostered, also, by a lack of parental love. When the relations between the child and the parents have been unhappy and when the parents have rejected the child, he may try to satisfy his need by grasping too early and at no matter what price at a love relationship which offers to fill the void.

A man who came to seek treatment because of a long-time and deep-seated inability to adjust to his marital situation showed these patterns very strikingly. He was at that time in his third marriage and the relationship was so disturbed that he feared that it too would break up. His work was always upset by his marital difficulties and as a result he had been much less successful than his capacities warranted. A relatively short time after each marriage he would get restless, uneasy and overactive. His powers of concentration would diminish and he would become uninterested in his work. He would also lose sexual interest in his wife. Then another woman would attract him. Though at first he would struggle against his feeling, his depression would increase and finally he would give way to his impulses.

His story was one of deprivation and rejection from his earliest years. His parents had been divorced when he was nine, and his mother had shown him little if any attention or affection after that. She had seen to it that he lived most of his life in schools and camps, and seen him only at the rarest intervals, when vacations necessitated it. He was always lonely and starved for affection. Neither was he successful or happy in the boy's way of life. A football to him was only something he was afraid of being hurt by. Consequently, he kept himself much to himself, but as soon as he was in his teens he began to feel a great interest in girls and what they stood for. It was not long before this drove him to direct expression. Very early, long before most of his associates were sexually active, he had developed a secret but nevertheless vigorous sexual life, involving one girl after another in rapid succession. Although these episodes eased his discomfort and made him feel stronger and more capable, they nevertheless always ended in disappointment and a return to the search for the ideal. His marriages, of course, were only a continuation of the same pattern. Treatment revealed that he had suffered such severe injury in childhood that he had never been able to elaborate for himself an assurance of his own manhood. It was this lack of belief in himself and his masculinity, and his overmastering need for love, that drove him along the path of constant search and disillusionment, for only new conquests could sustain his confidence in himself.

All along the way parents encounter difficulties in themselves. It may be hard to take the growing independence of their children and the widening separation that accompanies it. But it is a part of parenthood to prepare itself and the children for this final separation. It will be welcome or dreaded depending upon the parents' past relations to the children and upon the relations of the parents to each other. To those who have come to depend upon their children this will be a moment of deprivation against which they will struggle, and in their wish not to lose them, they may try to interfere with the social lives which those children are evolving. They have many anxieties for them, both conscious and unconscious, and out of their love they want to guide and help, to warn of pitfalls. They hope to spare their children the troubles and worries that they themselves encountered, to make sure that they find the happiness which the parents know is to be had. But in the last analysis, when all has been done that can be done, the young person must do his own growing up. There is the old saying, "*Si jeunesse savait*"—"If youth only knew." Perhaps—but if youth did know, there might be a great loss to the world in imagination and lofty adventure. Youth does not know and must find out for itself.

Nevertheless, parents will be missed if they pull away from the young in the mistaken belief that that is the way to give freedom, or because they feel resentful at being left out. Parents must be there ready and anxious to participate where the child wants participation, to accept all the confidence that the child is ready to give, to provide counsel and guidance where it can be accepted, and to produce the strong arm when it is obviously needed. Many times, when the path of the adolescent is buried under confusion and misdirection, an adult hand is going to be wanted. Often only parental strength and determination can provide the necessary weight and clarification—and when they are needed they are needed badly. There are times when only the word "no" will do. It takes a great deal of courage these days to voice that once innocent monosyllable. The reintroduction of it into the parental vocabulary is one of the crying needs of the parent-child relationship. The parent may hesitate for fear that he cannot make it stick or that he will lose the child's love and regard. Even this he will have to risk. The risk will not be great where the "no" comes from real love for the youngster and the determination not to let him damage himself by tackling more than he can handle. A parents' meeting was once galvanized when after a long discussion of the problems of managing late hours in boy-girl situations, one parent had the audacity to say, "I would not let my child get into such a situation." The meeting was at once astonished and refreshed by such a simple straightforward solution which smacked of heresy and old-fashioned authoritarianism. It had the merit of working.

It should be obvious that the path of the parent is a devious one, requiring the patience of Job and the wisdom of the serpent. But even more, it requires a willingness to see with the inner eye and understand with the heart. Parents who have been able to find their own solutions will be able to tolerate and accept the search that their children must make for their answers. They will be rewarded as the boy or girl emerges into a defined human being. In this human being, the excesses and variations will be pared away. The fluctuations will be less frequent, the attitudes and convictions more determined. The wide swings will be gone and more temperance and tolerance will characterize his enthusiasms. His choice of associates will stabilize and he will carve out for himself a place and a position, achieving a socialization of his impulses.

If his adult choices and convictions prove to be different from those of the parents, it must be remembered that the human animal differs from all others in the fact of his free development. He is not born with any fixed responses and his final development cannot be forecast as can that of a puppy dog or a heifer calf. Every human individual will develop differently from every other one. Variation is the most typical possession that the species has. This is the human thing; and successful parenthood means, above all, the ability to accept this human quality and to look with the eye of satisfaction upon the child's capacity to develop into an individual free of his early bondage and uniquely himself.

IV

The Adolescent and Himself

The central fact of every individual's life is his definition of himself. By the time maturity is reached this definition is fairly secure and stable. Everyone has an image of his physical self and an evaluation of the total "I." Feelings of adequacy or inadequacy, feelings of strength or weakness, feelings of physical attractiveness or lack of it, feelings of being intelligent or stupid, loved or unloved, secure or insecure are a continuing part of every individual's orientation. So too is his image of himself, however far from or close to reality it may be. More than this, he has a set of mental attitudes, beliefs and convictions, abhorrences and detestations which are also part of his identity. Everyone knows how tall he is, how small he is or how large he is, but the individual knows too whether he is a man or woman, a Democrat or a Republican, religious or irreligious. He is woven of a vast assortment of identifying data. Without it no one can operate in the world.

It was not always so. To the baby the world is himself and he is it. His powers embrace the universe that he knows. He is omnipotent and controls the world. During childhood he learns differently. Experience and training have already taught him his own limitations, his own feelings and their difference from those of others. He learns soon the limitations on his physical mastery. His physical safety depends upon this knowledge, as anyone can tell who has watched a baby walk calmly off the top step of a flight of stairs in complete ignorance of the fact that he will fall and hurt himself. Physical judgment must be supplemented by recognition of the separateness and identity of the mental self. This includes the recognition of one's thinking as one's own, not available to anyone else except as one wants to communicate it. It sounds simple to the adult who has long accepted it as an elementary fact. But it is knowledge acquired over a period of years and with considerable effort. Very young children don't have it at all. They believe that the world is managed by magic which emanates first from themselves and then from their omnipotent parents. They are convinced that those parents can read their thoughts. It is a discovery of some importance to the child to learn that his thoughts are his own and that he need not share them if he does not wish to. He can have a secret.

Throughout childhood, the physical changes are orderly and gradual so that adjustment to them is relatively simple. This is true too of the changes in the psychic life. But during adolescence growth is rapid, disorganized and chaotic. It is small wonder that the adolescent feels a stranger to himself—almost as if he were not the same person he has been through the years. And he isn't. He is changing in every smallest part of himself, at a rate and in a way which is far from easy, smooth, orderly or predictable. The changes are more than enough to disrupt his earlier assurance. Nothing stays put or in the same relation to other things that it has been. The body is temporarily unreliable. Getting used to the new body, both boys and girls will be tremendously preoccupied with it; nothing else will have equal importance. The attention they lavish on it is likely to seem fantastic to the adults around them, for they can spend seemingly any length of time considering themselves from all points of view. Hours of enraptured brooding seem to the parent, who is far too busy for such pleasures, just plain nonsense. Mirrors act as magnets, holding the young entranced. However, their self-fascination has a purpose: it helps the youngster to be sure of who and what he is, and of the acceptability of that identity. It is funny and foolish and touching and charming.

At adolescence, the problems of boys and girls, including the nature of their concern with their bodies, begin to reflect the marked sex difference that is the main point of their development. Boys necessarily are most anxious to grow up to match the picture of the perfect male. This picture lays great emphasis on body size and build. He must be tall. That is obvious. A small man is far less desirable than a tall one. Anyone who can read the daily newspaper knows that. He must be strong and powerful. Well-developed muscles are much admired and every boy will fear himself inferior if his are small. Height, weight, strength—these are legitimate concerns, for their satisfactory development will prove to the doubtful young boy that he is going to be a satisfactory man—as good as or better than others. Since that is precisely what all the growing is about, there isn't any reason why he shouldn't be absorbed in it. Naturally, he is likely to be afraid it isn't going to go along as it should: that maybe he will be too much this or too little that. In line with his interest in his physical development, sports now become of top importance because they give the boy the chance to prove himself in competition with his contemporaries. Some youngsters seem to be interested in nothing but sports and their parents despair of getting them to take a serious view of anything else. Studies are shoved aside for the much more vital physical life.

In all this absorption in the physical self the boy's deepest concern has to do with masculinity. The strong and powerful, heavily muscled body seems desirable to him precisely because people regard these exterior body traits as indices of the powerful masculinity which he is seeking. For the boy the question of his sexual development cannot be evaded;

it is too obvious. The first hallmarks of the male—changes in voice and beard—are apparent to everyone. Underneath all is his interest in the growth of his sexual organ. One of the most common anxieties, even in grown men, concerns the adequacy of the genital itself, for it is here that the essential maleness is located. It is almost a folklore that a large genital is particularly desirable. Smallness is associated with incompetence. Unconsciously, the boy wants to be sure he will be as effective as the father whom as a tiny child he envied and despaired of rivaling, for at that time his father's genital appeared incredibly large to him. For this reason, some boys find it hard to believe that their own genitals are adequate even when there is no possible reason for doubting it. Then, too, the common activities of boys' lives make it almost impossible for them to avoid comparison of their bodies in general and their genital equipment in particular. The resultant rivalry is sometimes expressed indirectly through trials of strength and competitive athletics, or it may find expression in direct comparison and, in earlier adolescence, in competitive masturbation, where not only the size of the organ but its function can be displayed. For girl and boy alike, it is essential to know that one is going to be capable, and therefore desirable sexually. For a boy the problem is especially pointed not only because of the greater obviousness of it but because of the nature of his role in later sexual life. Potency is a question of such overmastering importance to adolescent boys that it often clouds a great deal else. Sometimes the doubts and the anxiety— the overmastering need to prove that one is a man—are the underlying cause of premature sexual activity or what appears to be sexual delinquency.

The boy's attitude toward himself and his vitally important body will often be completely unrealistic. Differences between himself and others so insignificant as to be nearly non-existent will be picked up and magnified out of all relation to reality. He may develop the idea that his body is ridiculously large or small, that he is doomed to become a freak because of these defects and his horrifying difference from others. Or he may be sure he is going to be a midget, and give himself up for lost. No amount of reassurance will help and he may simply have to live with his fears until it is proved that his forebodings aren't true.

Another aspect of his self-fascination is his preoccupation with his dress. Although boys' clothes afford less scope for their concern than do girls', they exploit what possibilities there are to the fullest. They become crotchety, fussy, dissatisfied, fearful that they will not be dressed to the last detail in accordance with the prevailing requirements. The shirt, the tie, the slacks are all subject to searching scrutiny lest they vary in some minute but vastly dangerous particular from what is accepted and therefore proper. The persuasion or advice of parents in these momentous matters is likely to be ineffective. The boy is his own court of last appeal, and has most decided notions of his own. Something, oh heavens, is too sissy; something else is impossible, nobody wears such things; but this is indispensable because everybody else has it. Everything is potentially a uniform, a badge, a guarantee of acceptance and an assertion of correctness or the stigma of a social outcast.

In all this the boy is obviously associating his clothes with himself; with them he is attempting to achieve the physical appearance he considers desirable, to assure himself that he is like everybody else and therefore entirely acceptable.

Sometimes, at this age, a youngster will develop a tendency to worry about his health. He may get a notion that he is developing a disease or a defect of some sort. Headaches, digestive upsets, heart diseases or some mysterious ailment that nobody can track down, are the usual choices. In all probability there will not be the slightest reason for his concern, but that won't change his attitude. If he becomes really deeply disturbed, it may indicate that he is dealing with some inner difficulty which should be investigated. If after an examination and negative report by his doctor, the boy still cannot believe that there is nothing the matter with him, he almost certainly has some emotional disturbance which needs attention.

This is not a matter to be neglected. A persistent fancy of this kind is at the least an indication of an inner conflict and anxiety, and it may represent the early stages of serious emotional disorder. A boy of fifteen began to show these symptoms by complaining that he was sure he had heart disease. He had pain when he exerted himself and sometimes he would have attacks of what appeared to be collapse, with rapid pulse, pallor and sweating. He began to take excessively good care of himelf, going to bed at absurdly early hours, following a rigid, health-building diet and abstaining from all vigorous activity. He was preoccupied with his weight and height, the color of his skin and all the minute details of his physical being which seemed to him to indicate health or disease. He was a tall, well-built boy for his age and his fears seemed clearly absurd. At first his parents were inclined to "laugh it off" and tease him a little about being a hypochondriac. But when his complaints persisted and he began to insist upon staying home from school they took him to their family doctor. Here it was quickly discovered that he had no physical complaints and was on the contrary a robust, normal boy. When this discovery failed to reassure him and his symptoms persisted and even grew worse, it was concluded that his condition was emotional, and he was brought for psychiatric examination and treatment.

He was the middle child in a family of three, having an older sister and a younger brother. It was not possible to discover much of importance about his earlier years. He had always been a healthy child but he had been a little bit lost in the shuffle between his sister and his brother. He had always been a gentle and rather unaggressive boy, content to occupy himself with intellectual play rather than physical. Urging had induced him to take part in most of the school activities but it was never with great enthusiasm. His younger brother was a robust, vigorous and outgoing athlete and always the most popular boy in his group. The father had himself been a notable athlete in his college years and was outspoken in his determination that his sons should follow in his path. He gave the most obvious kind of approval to the younger boy, so the elder, feeling rejected by his father, turned to his mother for companionship and solace. It appeared that he had early given up the struggle to win his father's approval and had gone his somewhat solitary and wounded way.

Adolescence was a deep trial to this boy, who felt in no way prepared to tackle the problems of masculinity. He longed for the love and support of his father and therefore for the love and protection of all men and boys. This characteristic aroused in him a great deal of anxiety because it had a certain homosexual coloration. Contacts with boys therefore became more and more difficult, especially the physical contacts of the dressing room, the gymnasium, the shower and the swimming pool. As his conflict grew in intensity, he could find no solution except to express it through the anxiety about his body which his symptoms justified. His predicament lay in the fact that if he allowed himself to follow his deepest longing and find companionship and love in boys, he was in danger of developing homosexual feelings for them. If he withdrew from them, he was faced with the agonizing feelings of inadequacy and inferiority. He was a failure. Clearly there was no out from such a conflict except to find its sources and help him understand them and build his never-developed confidence in himself.

To add to the general confusion that characterizes adolescence, the age at which boys mature varies greatly. Some will be small and still childish at an age when others will already have done considerable growing. A result of this is that the child whose development is out of line with the majority of his group is apt to be excluded. The little fellow will be unable to keep up with the bigger ones and the great big boy will feel like a misfit with the smaller ones. Also beard growth and voice change occur at different times in different boys. Some will still be the "beardless youth" while others will be wielding a razor or nearly ready to. The response of the boy to these signs of sexual development is something of an index to his feelings about becoming a man. Some of them choose to disregard it and refuse, for example, to shave until a great deal of pressure is put on them. Others anticipate the necessity of shaving by beginning before there is any possible need for it. This last youngster is eager for his new self and watching for it with excitement and pleasure.

The girl is proverbially even more concerned with her body than is the boy, although in this there is more proverb than truth. She is certainly no less preoccupied but probably no more so. The point with her is that her concern has many more avenues for expression. No less than her brother, she is going to require of herself correspondence with some real or fancied ideal of feminine perfection. Sometimes this will be her mother but often it will be another person—a teacher perhaps, or an accomplished older girl who possesses the qualities or physical characteristics that the youngster longs for. Nowadays, there are some pretty explicitly physical requirements—more likely than not to be embodied in the reigning Hollywood queen—which determine whether or not a girl is acceptable. For example, it is now apparently a settled fact that girls can be tall, though not too tall, and preferably quite thin. There is no particular penalty attached to being small, but to be fat is a disaster which often causes intense agony. The girl who is much taller than the average may also suffer keenly. These youngsters may develop feelings amounting almost to despair and in many instances will be so defeated by what they regard as their disastrous deformity that they will prefer to withdraw from all social intercourse rather than attempt the competition in which they feel they are doomed to failure. Their depression may be great enough not only to upset their social activities but to damage their school achievement so that a youngster who has been a good student may begin to fail.

This is precisely what happened to one youngster whom I knew, a very tall girl who had been such a brilliant student that her parents and teachers had allowed themselves to build high hopes for her. When she began to fall behind in her studies, her distress was obvious. She didn't seem to want to participate in any of the usual recreations of her friends and became more and more withdrawn and quite clearly unhappy; finally she asked to be allowed to leave school. This was absurd with her record. When she walked into the clinic, it was easy to see what was going on. She hung her head and stooped to try to conceal her really unusual height. Her dress was carefully designed to make her inconspicuous. She was in absolute desperation, bewildered by her growth and uncertain of who she was. Her younger sister was, in her eyes, ideal, but for her own part she had no hope of being acceptable either to herself or to others. Unable to keep up with the speed of her own development, she had decided to give up the struggle, retire from the world and bury herself out of sight, as she imagined everyone must be wanting her to do. All her other talents meant nothing to her at the moment. Her life was over. Some months later, as others began to catch up to her, she had with help absorbed the picture of herself; even though she still was larger than most of her contemporaries, she was beginning to feel comfortable with herself.

In the course of their development both boy and girl have to do a great deal of copying and conforming. If one hasn't a settled self inescapably one's own, one has to acquire it by taking over a self that is uniformly acceptable. In girls, this necessity may show itself in a particular preoccupation with clothes. Some of them seem never to be satisfied with the way they manage to dress. No matter how parents try to give the girl everything she seems to want, nothing is ever right. What the girl longed for and "couldn't live without" one day is discarded as being impossible the next. Even if the family decides that she is to buy her own clothes, making her own unchecked selections, she will still have the same difficulty—which, of course, has nothing to do with her clothes and everything to do with her inability to accept herself and her own body.

All parts of the girl's body will be to her of pressing significance. Feet and hands; legs, their size and shape; neck, buttocks, especially if they seem too large. Breasts, of course, are of transcendent importance, for to the girl they are the distinctive and final credential of her desirable femininity. Her body contains within the real proof of her satisfactory femininity but that proof cannot be so easily tested.

Most of the time there is reasonable conformity to the expected, but sometimes a minor deviation will loom so large in a girl's mind that she will show an almost ridiculous amount of anxiety. If there is actually some fairly marked divergence, the situation may become acute. In either case the mother will be very wise to take the matter with due seriousness. If the girl's worry is actually baseless, intelligent reassurance will usually do the trick. But if the difficulty is real, positive action must be taken. Breasts that are extremely small, for instance, are a reasonable source of disturbance, but in the matter of appearance they are more easily dealt with than breasts that are unusually large. In the last case proper clothing will usually take care of the situation. It must be remembered that today everything is known and measured and there is a slavish adoration of what is presumed to be "normal." To be sure, there isn't any such thing, but everybody strives for it nonetheless.

The physical with its special pressure in the direction of the sexual is, of course, not the only preoccupation of children of this age and it will be superseded by others. The appraisal of one's self and the location of one's self in the surrounding world is a problem of growth which begins in very simple form in early childhood and continues until maturity is achieved. The questions, Who am I? Where do I belong? What do I believe in? What can I do? What is my value to others and theirs to me? What are my powers? are all to be answered in this period of life with some degree of finality. It is particularly with the philosophical questions that the adolescent will concern himself; his relation to the universe and to the society in which he lives are of prime concern. The answers are a long time coming, and some people never really arrive at them. But adolescence is the period when there is an effort to find them. The problems of ethics and morals, of politics as well as religion, are important to the child at this time.

These problems have to be settled within the youngster himself, for he has as yet no arena in which to act out his aspirations, his ideals and his ambitions. Of necessity he must resort to reflection and fantasy. This is the age then of daydreams and imagination. Before anything is *done*, it must be pondered deeply, looked at from all sides, inspected, turned over, considered and reconsidered. In his reflection the youngster will be drawn within himself and he is likely to remain withdrawn long hours at a time. One mother expressed herself as completely bewildered by the fact that her fifteen-year-old daughter seemed to be not at all bored to come home from school, throw herself flat on her back in her room and lie there gazing at the ceiling hours on end. It all seemed a great waste of time to the mother, but no amount of urging could persuade the maiden that this was so. She was "thinking" and she continued to think for many months. She was thinking to good purpose, and when she was through she was more settled and sure and more comfortable with herself than she had been before. Parents may complain that there is the world's work to be done and no time for dawdling. But this is not dawdling. This is important work, and every youngster will have to do it to test in his mind the beliefs, the feelings, the drives and ambitions which he is later going to act upon.

His experience in regard both to the world around him and to his own powers makes this process necessary. Any adult faced with a new and unpredictable circumstance— whether it be moving to a new part of the world, taking a new job, going into a hospital for an operation or having a baby for the first time—attempts to take care of his anxiety by finding out all he can about it, planning for it as carefully as possible and living it through beforehand. The same is true on a much larger scale of the youngster who knows nothing of what life can bring or how he can cope with it.

One conspicuous element of this brooding daydream life is ambition. The adolescent has begun to consider his life interests and goals. They are probably lofty and even unreal, but he is impatient to achieve them and the rewards that come with them. It will be a long time and a hard struggle before his ambitions can be realized, but in daydreams he can have them all and have them at once. Nothing is simpler than in fantasy to roam the seven seas as a masterful explorer, to enchant great audiences with one's incomparable art, to stampede one's opponents with matchless oratory, to heal the sick with incomparable skill, to demolish one's antagonists with invincible power and finally to be crowned the chief citizen of the world. One boy spent a great deal of time by himself playing records and conducting the orchestras there recorded. His mother, a woman of reasonably curious disposition, had a natural question about his prolonged musical sessions. She investigated and found him giving a reasonably good imitation of Toscanini. Having forgotten her own days of bettering Duse, she was convinced the boy was mad. She called his father, having visions of the prompt arrival of those who would take charge of the mentally deranged. There was considerable confusion and anguish during which the boy became more and more sheepish and more and more inarticulate. He could not answer any of the questions about why he did it except to say that he "felt like it." Happily it did not take long for common sense to assert itself, and the boy returned to his ambitious dreaming.

Love also is the subject of prolonged fantasy. Here the loved one is properly responsive if not eager. Here there are no rebuffs, no rejections, no lost loves. Here is a world of ineffable bliss where love is matched with love, beauty is an unquestioned possession, and the youngster sails from glory to glory bathed in a rosy light. A good many of these dreams go further and take the youngster on to his ultimate objective. They involve home and business, family and responsibility. A large proportion of girls imagine themselves having and caring for babies. This is eminently natural, since it represents at once something for which the girl longs and about which she has some uneasiness. To imagine it, to dream about it, is to live through and to achieve some mastery over it.

As the dreams continue, the youngster will carry them over into the family setting. The boy will one day be the desperate Hamlet, the next a competent man of affairs;

one day head in the air, the next down to earth. Masterful-
ness will give way to doubt and indecision. Part of the
time the girl will be all co-operation and consideration; at
other times she will be far beyond the mundane and vulgar
considerations of practical life.

Any parent who lets himself believe that each of these
postures is final is going to need considerable mental agility
and is likely to suffer from mental fatigue. To keep up with
the youngsters' changes at this time is quite a trick. A high
degree of philosophical calm and a well-developed sense of
humor, along with basic understanding, are to be highly
recommended. The adolescent may often be secretive but
he is really crystal clear to those who can understand his
actions and their meaning. To identify and accept himself,
to come to terms with the person that he is, after discovering *who* that person is, is really the purpose of all this
struggle. Naturally, all parents will want to help their
youngsters and the youngsters will want help. But most of
the job the child has to do himself, making use of the kind
of help which comes from his relationships. These are of
the greatest importance, for in the give and take of human
relations the youngster can find a sense of security and self-
esteem, a sense of strength in himself, and a belief in his
ability to deal with the complex inner problems he must
solve.

The watchwords for the parents are tolerance, acceptance,
patience and humor. They must stand by to be there when
they are wanted and needed, to provide a sounding board for
the exploring youngster and a corrective when he seems
to be wandering too far afield. Provided with an environment which gives him a good relationship with his parents
and understanding and respect, the youngster will find the
strength he needs to deal with himself and arrive at a sure
sense of his own inner identity.

V

The Adolescent in the Family

Up to this point we have been discussing and trying to clarify the mechanics and structure of adolescent development. Our attempt now will be to show how the various forces at work within the child are expressed in his relations with others. The home, of course, is the principal setting, and the family the first to observe and be affected by the child's changing attitudes.

Of the family, it is usually the mother who first notices and is disturbed by the change in her previously delightful and satisfactory child. She has probably become accustomed to a fairly orderly and accountable youngster, not too much given to back talk or other troublesome kinds of behavior. He has shown some willingness to accept the family circle as one in which he was able to be happy and to adjust and has not been excessively critical of its members. He could be expected to arrive at the family doorstep at approximately the hour he indicated or that was suggested. He may even have accepted a suggestion that an occasional bath or general putting to rights of his person and his belongings would not be beneath one of his elevated station. He has become fairly well adjusted to the idea that he could take care of his clothes and quarters without losing caste, and would even consider the possibility that he could participate in family dish-washing without altogether compromising himself.

In those years between babyhood and adolescence there

has been a sense that all was right with the child and the child was right with his world. He has been functioning well and a pleasure both to himself and to those around him. He has seemed happy. He has been able to meet with composure all the demands that have been made of him. During those years parents often have a comfortable sense of relaxation and relief. Infancy with all of its dramatic episodes was taxing, and the days of childhood seem like quiet waters. But with the beginning of adolescence, these halcyon days are over and days of trial are ahead, days that are sometimes troubled, occasionally agonizing, often delightful and always exciting.

Familiarity with the varied and complex drives of adolescence, which we have already explored, should make clear why it is and must be first of all within the family circle that the drama of adolescence is acted out. For until and unless maturity is accomplished here, it cannot be accomplished at all. The initial need is to assert some sort of freedom from family control and domination.

Up to now the youngster has been safely contained within the family circle. Now he must begin the process of breaking out of that circle. At first he is apt to display not much more than a determined opposition where formerly he showed compliance. The relied-upon family dishwasher may quite suddenly develop a vast indifference to his usual routines. Many are the bewildered mothers who wail, "I can't get that child to do a thing in the house." Mother's little helper has given way to someone who appears never to have heard of such a thing as family co-operation. He or she now much prefers matters of such singular importance as club meetings, lolling in a comfortable chair, talking over the telephone interminably, to the drab and uninteresting concerns of the household. Attempts to remedy this situation by the formerly reliable methods of persuasion and discipline may not bear the expected fruit. Evasion and delay are useful tools. The watchword of this method is "Just a minute" or "I'll do it when I finish." The tally of the verbal ways to avoid going along with a parental request is almost endless. Some parents announce themselves as driven to distraction by a noticeable tendency on the part of the young to develop deafness at convenient moments. To make a request half a dozen times and then be met with an apparently surprised "Were you talking to me?" has been known to flurry the calm of even the best-tempered. Naturally, "I'm busy" is a gambit of such ordinary quality that it is rarely used and then only in extreme cases. Homework may become a fascinating undertaking if only it interferes with doing something that the parent requires. This high devotion to intellectual labor is a common method of escape. Not infrequently when the parent has bowed his head to the obvious necessity of following the call to higher endeavor, he has later discovered the "homework" to consist of elaborate manicuring, shoe-polishing, bemused gazing in the mirror or just plain sitting and doodling. Brought to book, the child takes recourse in the esoteric "I'm thinking." Parents may wonder at times why all the "thinking" done by adolescent youngsters has not by now solved the problems of the universe. It has done a lot toward it.

If such methods as these do not avail, it is probable that the child will display some open hostility. It is safe to say that at some time during adolescence parents may expect to encounter real enmity from their youngsters. What only yesterday was cherished and admired is today scorned and despised. This includes the home and all within it. Nothing will be spared. One youngster will insist that the house or apartment is impossibly out of taste and shabby. Surely he is not to be expected to entertain his friends in such surroundings. Another will announce that his entire social position is being threatened by the old family car, and he for one would rather stay home than be seen in it. He will at one time or another discover that other families have different attitudes and different manners, and he will be quite sure that these are superior to his own. Girls will display, very often, extreme disapproval of the dress and behavior of their parents, greeting mother with the cheerful remark, "You're certainly not going out of the house in that thing, are you?" The manner in which the various members of the family conduct themselves is cause for derision or anguish. The table manners of the younger members are certainly not to be borne, much less to be exposed to the associates of these fastidious young. That is a horror which, they will aver, no one could seriously expect them to endure. The most minute detail of household management will come under devastating scrutiny and every fault, largely imagined, will be hauled to the light and inspected with a view to remedying it.

All these signs of defiance and estrangement are going to be confusing unless they are understood and a sense of humor about them is strenuously cultivated. For a mother who has been her son's and daughter's unquestioned mentor to find herself consigned to the doghouse is not a comfortable experience. The constant criticism of family standards can be exasperating beyond the ability of anyone who hasn't met it to understand. "You don't expect me to have my friends in this old barn, I hope" is scarcely the kind of statement that the parents who have a kind of lingering fondness for "the old barn" are going to appreciate. To be received with airs of superiority which, upon being punctured, yield up such nuggets as "Well, no one around this place has any real intellect" is a choice experience, but scarcely cheering. There will often be a studied attempt to make over the parents, but it is unlikely that after renovation they will be any more acceptable than they were before; for they can't stop being parents and there's the rub. Of course, it is a corollary to all this that the manners, appearances, and general conduct of others' parents are above reproach. If one could just be like the so-and-so's, all would be well. Frantic attempts to conform will lead straight to the pit, for they won't work and there will be next week's list of disasters to deal with.

Parents will react to this situation in various ways, ranging from violent determination to bring the youngster to book, to a kind of lackadaisical acceptance of whatever is done and an indulgence of every whim. Generally there is a hopeful balance between the two extremes and some sort of reconciliation to the changing young person is accomplished.

A horrified parent in asking for an appointment had given every sign of being faced with a serious emergency. To her it was. She was stricken by the fact that her young daughter, who was only thirteen, had announced in icy and venomous tones, "I hate you." This came from a child who had, up to the time of puberty, been a model of deportment and a pleasure to all. However, there were signs here and there of less than ideal adjustment, though she had never shown any striking behavior difficulties. School had been a pleasure to her and she to it. She had been a bookish child from her early years, but since the parents were bookish there seemed no particular reason to take exception to this. She had never had a large number of friends but had devoted herself to one or two children with whom she was unusually compatible. The mother's story was that for the year preceding the horrid event which brought her for help there had been progressive difficulty. The little girl had early begun to make demands for privileges which the parents felt were inappropriate to her age, and when denied she had withdrawn from the family group and become sullen and petulant. The issue which brought on the outbreak was apparently a trivial one having to do with hours and limitations on her freedom. The mother had, with the father's co-operation, and even urging, insisted upon continuing to treat the youngster as a child. There was very little family consultation and the youngster's views were not given consideration nor discussed in the family councils.

More careful investigation began to show various other defects in the parents' attitude toward the girl. She was one of three children, having two younger brothers. The boys were easier for the mother to deal with, as she herself said. She had not been well prepared for the first child and to some extent had resented having her. The conflict between the mother and daughter had really begun during the oedipal stage when the mother's resentment of the little girl's femininity began to appear. When the trials and tribulations of adolescence began, the mother failed to give the youngster the kind of help to establish herself which was needed. She paid little attention to the youngster's appearance and continued to "dress her" as a little girl. The mother was a strict formalist and could not endure the bad manners which the youngster had displayed in the year preceding. Through all of this the young girl felt deeply that she was struggling for her rights to femininity and that her mother was trying to deprive her of them. So, inevitably, "I hate you."

This kind of resistance and antagonism is not permanent. Happily it gives way to its opposite. There is a complete *volte-face* and again *a reasonable* citizen sits at the family board. Family practices and family faces are again acceptable. Smaller brothers and sisters will be approved. There will be every sign of loyalty to the family as it is, which, apparently, at this point could not be bettered. Often the youngster will return to ways of behaving that are reminiscent of earlier days. He is once again a child, even at times a baby. He turns again to his parents for support, guidance and love, and as might be expected is quite willing to love in exchange. Once again he is the "good child," out of reach, for the moment, of the dangers and anxieties that plague his footsteps when he is on his more determined path of growing up. Now "I love you. You are the best mother in the world," or "Daddy, you are marvelous" have taken the place of "I hate you." This state of affairs is usually welcomed by those around him, and there is rejoicing as at the prodigal's return.

Sometimes the return is more than is bargained for. In the first place, the changeability itself is disturbing and alarming to parents. There is no way of knowing what to expect. The sooner parents learn that and accept it as part and parcel of the situation, the sooner will they be able to adjust to things as they are. But the immediate changes are nevertheless disturbing. Moreover, in his zeal for giving up his old rebellion and returning to the ways of his childhood the youngster may show a decided tendency to overdo it. For example, they often display a most remarkable disregard of cleanliness and tidiness. It may take the combined efforts of the entire family to get the devastating Beau Brummell into the bathtub. It is not uncommon to find the "young lady" (as she thinks of herself) appearing for her evening celebration dressed in all her glory with a magnificently dirty neck around which she has draped her pearls. As for personal belongings, the place for them is the floor. Any household that has missed the three-ring circus that is put on when the daughter goes into a panic because she cannot find her finest apparel (because it is in a heap under the bed) has not known real hilarity.

Here we see the youngster doing two things at once—acting like a baby, being dirty and disorderly and irresponsible, yet displaying other attitudes that are consistent with his age. Sometimes he is even more thorough in his reversion to childhood. Abandoning momentarily the drive toward independence, desiring only to remain in the family and enjoy the security and satisfaction of parental love, he may make all the old demands on his parents, turn to them for direction and guidance in every detail, and seem utterly unable to do for himself. Mixed with the dismay produced by this tendency of the adolescent to go backward in his development is often a certain satisfaction. The mother feels as if she were getting back the child she so much loved and enjoyed; the father is happy to see his youngster once more quiet and orderly and to be relieved of the recurrent "problems." The child's greater willingness to confide, and his amiability and compliance combine to flatter and elevate the parents' sense of their importance in his life.

But neither does this last. Harmony again gives way to rebellion; co-operation becomes again a thing of the past. Admittedly, these changes are difficult to take. In order to be tolerated at all, they must be seen as two different phases of a unified process which follows not a straightforward but an alternately backward and forward course. The rapidity with which these changes occur is also upsetting. In one day or even an hour there may be repeated shifts of mood and attitude. Not until the issue of maturity is solved will periods of disturbance and rebellion be a thing of the past.

Along with the negative attitudes with which the now thoroughly confused parents have to deal there are also a great many positive demands and exactions. The number of things without which the life of a teen-ager is sure to wither and become a dreadful wasteland can be truly formidable. In the case of the girl, one of the first things on the list is clothes. Her need will seem a bottomless pit; this, coupled with her complete lack of care for what is provided, is apt to produce a parental explosion. A costume for this moment, a new dress, suit, hat, bag, permanent, and what have you is the order of the day. At times one will wonder if the girl believes that the entire family income is to be placed at her disposal. And keeping up with the Joneses! The necessity to have what any other youngster in the group has, it will soon be discovered, is absolute. This is the period during which parents are likely to report that Jane is so selfish that no one could possibly believe it. She thinks only of herself and makes demands regardless of their logic or possibility.

The boy isn't very far behind his sister in his demands. They may differ from hers but they are there. Perhaps there is a sudden need for elaborate equipment for some undertaking which is likely to last all of a week. Today a clarinet and tomorrow a cello. An expensive camera may appear to be as important as regular meals. Later on, in some areas, a car acquires just that importance to both boys and girls. The author has talked to many boys and girls who have felt that not to have a car is like being afflicted with some terrible disfiguring disease which cuts you off from your fellows. Besides, it has a considerable bearing on one's position in the group. Those with cars are much more apt to be sought after than those without.

Money is a central source of anguish in the home at this time. The notion that there is a delightful well somewhere from which one can dredge up all needed cash seems at times to bewitch the adolescent mind. The tormented cry of the breadwinner, "Do you think I am *made* of money?" is all too familiar. One is reminded of the fourteen-year-old who was found to be going through thirty dollars a week for such vital necessities as cakes and sodas. Her parents were dumbfounded when they discovered that she had managed to convince and cajole them into thinking that all this was necessary and without it she would be next door to starvation. This attitude toward money represents not only the inexperience and the essential naïveté of the young person; it is also an expression of a wish for the days of childhood when one never had to know the source of anything, for parents were omnipotent and represented infinite wells of satisfaction. Responsibility, then, was a word unknown.

Co-operation is always a thought that appeals in the business of parent-child relationships. But co-operation may at times be a spot difficult to get. The parent may suggest in all reason that "if everybody will get together to do the chores around the house, we'll all be able to spend less time at them and then we can do what we want." It's fair for everyone to do his share of the work for his share of the benefits. It's a generally admired notion, and it may come as something of a surprise that it isn't always met with delight by the growing young. The chances are that there won't be too much carry-through even if lip service is given.

There is no greater artist at evasion than the young person in his teens. It is all agreed that family tasks will be done on some arranged basis. The girl will help in those things best suited to her abilities and the boy with the things that he can do. Everyone will take care of his own quarters and possessions. Certainly, why not? Moreover, it is no more than sensible that mother should be able to get a helping hand with the general assembly job of food and laundry and such like. That's settled, then. Nevertheless, the parent should not be surprised at the number of times he will discover that the entire business has been skipped. Clothes all over the floor; bathroom left as if a retiring army had just been through it; personal belongings strewn from front door to back. A suggestion that this wasn't in the agreement will bring a surprised, "Oh, I forgot" or "I'll do it as soon as I get back from the game" or "I haven't time now, I've got to go." A request for a hand with some task brings the helpful response, "In a minute." If all the minutes that adolescents had claimed for themselves in these circumstances were available, we should have a nice assortment of light years on hand.

What makes all this bearable and even largely a pleasure is that these exasperating demonstrations are interspersed with others which are, at the opposite extreme, delightful. Smiling calm and amiability will prevail. Nothing will be too much or too difficult. Parents will suddenly find themselves the objects of devoted admiration and unquestioned obedience. Yesterday's young lady of fashion, whose most urgent need was to be arrayed in all the splendor possible, is today's maiden about to take the veil. All solicitude and renunciation, she will rush to her mother's help and insist that everything can be left to her, no one is to do a thing, she will get the meal and do all that is necessary. Her mother is just to rest. There may be some question in the mother's mind whether she has aged so terribly in the last few days or is as near the grave as these attentions would indicate, but she needn't worry; let her relax and enjoy the charm of the girl caught in the grip of her need to be again her parents' "good child." A daughter has no corner on such acts of grace and mercy. Sons are just as apt to show a sudden and inexplicable willingness to undertake all sorts of domestic horrors which even to contemplate last week made them violent. These times of Eden-like calm bring a joy into the youngster's relations all the way around. He has reached some sort of plateau. He has solved something. He is at home in the world and at peace with everybody. Perhaps he has discovered a strength in himself which will allow him to stop rebelling for the time being.

Younger brothers and sisters also have a role to play vis-à-vis the adolescent, though it is not so important as the parents'. For along with the other changes in the adolescent is a change in his attitude toward the younger members of his family. A mixture of supercilious contempt and disapproval often colors his real love and devotion. He may even demand to be given certain authority over the younger children—that is, to begin acting out a parental role. But his capriciousness and unpredictability make the situation difficult for the younger child. At one moment the grown-up brother or sister will be all helpfulness, anxious to give advice and to promote the advancement of the younger one; at the next moment, he may be evincing an attitude of severe dis-approval and rejection. Although this constantly shifting state of affairs cannot fail to confuse and often upset the younger child, it has its merits too. Older brothers and sisters are invaluable assets. The fact that they are closer to the young child in age than his parents creates a strong bond of sympathy; the younger sees in his older brother or sister an ideal toward which he can easily strive. Also, parental feelings and attitudes can be expressed through the older child, against whom it is far more difficult for the young ones to rebel than against the parents. In many homes the older brothers and sisters can accomplish much that parents have difficulty in handling.

One of the most difficult manifestations of the adolescent age to deal with is the burgeoning interest in the opposite sex. About this there is very apt to be some disagreement between the youngster and his elders. The deeper and more extensive problems of the sexual behavior of adolescent boys and girls will be discussed in detail in a later chapter. Here it will be enough to point out the most obvious effects upon family living and family adjustments. First of all, of course, there is the problem of parental acceptance of the new phenomenon. When the child announces in all sorts of ways that he or she is now preparing to make a start in the difficult world of boy-and-girl relations, parents must of necessity have some reaction to it. They may regard it as a shocking exhibition of the youngster's wish to anticipate privileges which should not come until later. They may wel-come it as a sign of maturity. But however this new develop-ment is received, it will require adjustment on the part of the family. They will have to become reconciled to the underlying fact that the new interest foretells the day when the youngster will leave the parental home for the larger world and a family of his own.

This may be inevitable and expected, but it is by no means

always desired or accepted. For most parents it is a fact that it is hard to part with the child and accept the grown-up. But they had best recognize that in the course of the growing up of their children they themselves come to depend much more than they realize upon the love that those children give them. This situation has long been acknowledged to be a stumbling block in parent-child relations. It varies in its importance depending upon how well the parents have adjusted to their own roles and to each other. Some sense of loss can scarcely be avoided and is to be expected. The mother is likely to feel it more than the father. In all probability, in today's family, it is she who has had the lion's share of the chore of upbringing. Fathers are too often forced into secondary position as parents. Consequently it is the mother who more frequently develops an exaggerated dependence upon her children and suffers a corresponding loss when the time for separation comes.

The symptoms of awakening interest in the opposite sex are first apparent in the family. The youngster who seems to her parents still a little girl is likely to announce that it is high time she adopted lipstick, nylon stockings, girdles and party dresses. Her brother does not require such spectacular signs of his availability. The day of formal adoption of long trousers passed when small boys of two began to wear them. Naturally much will depend on the practices of the community or even the part of the community with which the child is associated. For it is certain that whatever "everybody else is doing" will be what finally determines the manner of the youngster's initiation. This is the age when the need to belong, to be part of a known group, to identify oneself with a group is of first-class importance. The slogan is: "Everyone else is doing it, I don't see why I can't."

The author had rather amusing evidence of this upon receiving within a short space of time a letter from each of two youngsters in the same community, both making the same assertion and seeking help in the redress of the same wrong. Both writers stated that "everyone was being allowed to go out except themselves," and asked the author to intervene on their behalves with their parents. The obvious conclusion was that the maidens had somewhat exaggerated their plight. That argument, however, is one of the most powerful weapons the young person has and one that will have great influence with his parents. For parents too will often find that they are not unaffected by this need to conform, and will be uneasy if their children don't follow with the general pattern. But whatever the child's demand, whether it be permission to "date" (an institution that will be discussed more extensively later) or freedom to dictate his own hours, dress, or social life, it is all part of the same demonstration of his determination to begin solving the problem of his sexual life.

All of this can cause a great uproar in the home. At first the parents may resist strongly and attempt to control and regulate the whole business out of existence. This most certainly will not work. Then may follow a reluctant concession here and there, with the firm intention of seeing that things go no further. But unless parents actually have a guiding philosophy on which they themselves can rely, there is a good possibility that the youngster will manage to bring about whatever he or she decides on. It all seems to be done by a process of erosion and gradual wear and tear which breaks down parental resistance. At the same time the parents are getting used to the idea that ultimately the youngster must have his freedom.

Now is the time when the relationship that has been built between the parents and the children shows its strength or weakness. The mother's attitudes particularly play a large role. This is not because the role of the father is unimportant but because so often the mother's role has been dominant. She may, at this point, develop feelings of jealousy and rivalry toward her daughter. No matter how odious this idea may seem, it is a not uncommon fact of mother-daughter relationships. The symptoms of this malady are various and depend upon whether the mother attempts to bury her feelings and thereby protect herself from knowledge that it exists, or whether she makes it all too apparent. But no matter what the symptoms, the underlying facts will be clear to the girl and she will react to them unhappily one way or another. It is usually the fact that women who now exhibit jealousy of their daughters have never actually accepted them or really wished them to enjoy the privileges and satisfactions of adult womanhood. The old saying, "A daughter is a daughter to the end of her life," only tells half of the story. It omits to say that a daughter is a rival from the beginning of her life. And rivals are seldom accepted calmly or affectionately. For an insecure and immature woman to face the fact that her daughter is growing up to enjoy those allurements and romances which she herself has never stopped desiring is a painful task. She will respond with open or concealed hostility.

To illustrate this point, we can describe a young girl in exactly this position. Her mother left her father before she was born and had looked forward to her birth with nothing but apprehension and distress. Her conception had meant the end of her mother's girlhood without any recompense or satisfaction. Being forced to work, her mother had to make common cause with an aunt, who more than happily took over the youngster to make up to herself for her own loveless state. There was never any doubt that the mother rejected this small daughter, and no amount of conscientiousness and attention to the girl's physical and material welfare could conceal this fact. It was not long before the youngster responded by becoming troublesome and showing all sorts of difficult habits and disagreeable attitudes. As her mother said, "From the beginning she was a problem.

No matter what I did for her, it never worked." When she was about ready for school the mother married again, and after a couple of years another small daughter was born who was greeted with much more love and satisfaction than our unhappy little girl had been. The situation only intensified her problems, making her even more unacceptable to her mother and her new father. Unsuccessful in school and unsuccessful in her play relations with other children, she developed many babyish tricks which, being misunderstood, only added to her own sense of being a misfit in her family and increased her mother's distress and discomfort.

When she entered adolescence she began very early to seek the attention of boys, and it was then that her mother began to show her intense rivalry. No matter what boy the girl brought home, the mother would immediately though unconsciously make every attempt to take her daughter's place with him. Since she had the obvious advantage of greater experience, she was more often than not successful, and the youngster would soon become aware that the boys she liked were more attached to her mother than to herself. This was the ultimate catastrophe in their relationship and brought out into the open the terrible conflict between them. As a final climax, the girl became pregnant. This was her answer to her mother's opposition. It was as if she knew that it was the only way in which she could finally assert her own femininity and win the struggle between herself and her mother, even though in winning she had to lose.

Although such tragic stories are not too frequent, difficulties arising from a distorted relationship between mother and daughter are not uncommon. One mother may oppose her daughter's growing up and be able to do nothing but depreciate and diminish her self-esteem. If the girl gives up under these attacks, the mother may reproach her with her failure. Another mother may wish to have her daughter anticipate her growing up so that she, the mother, may find again her own lost girlhood in her daughter's success. A mother of this kind is more than apt to abdicate her role. Exaggeratedly interested in the details of her daughter's life and too compliant with her often unwise desires, she will find herself unable to act as a wise guide and counselor or to supply the firm hand that is sometimes needed. She is inclined to justify her behavior by exhibiting a tremendous satisfaction in the fact that she and her daughter are just pals; she often says that no one could imagine them to be mother and daughter, they are so much like sisters. Such a state of affairs is surely out of joint and must inevitably be confusing and often deeply disturbing to the girl, who will find it much easier to free herself from a mother who plays the role of mother than from one who refuses to.

With their sons, women often establish relationships which react as unfavorably. The commonest source of difficulty is the mother's extreme attachment to her son and her unwillingness to relinquish him to another woman. There is the source of the proverbial antagonism between the daughter-in-law and mother-in-law, who are essentially rivals for the love of the same man. There cannot, of course, be any open opposition to the boy's attempts to move out into the world of girls. Only if the mother can hold him through love is she likely to succeed in preventing his onward rush toward maturity. She may and often does challenge his gallantry and show him her broken heart in a frantic attempt to hold on to him. There is no more subtle or deadly weapon than excessive love bringing with it excessive demand. Such a woman surrounds her son with a silken net of devotion and seduction, holding him, often without his own knowledge, tightly bound. The struggle for maturity is, as we have seen, difficult enough in itself; and if his mother opposes him, adding her weight to the forces pulling him back, he has little chance to succeed. He needs her free permission, even her encouragement, to carry on the difficult job of growing up. Without these he is fundamentally defeated, even though he may go on to give every appearance of success by marrying. Such marriages, however, often have a deadly defect at the core, arising from the strong attachment of these boys to their mothers and their inability wholly to free themselves for mature living. They may, and often do, marry girls who are thinly disguised mothers, ready to protect, dominate and control.

Boys of this kind were so commonly met with in the army that the whole situation became proverbial. There was widespread astonishment and resentment at the discovery that so many young men had been weakened and half-emasculated by maternal domination. By some it is even regarded as part of a generalized transitional situation in which women are becoming progressively more dominant and controlling. Certainly it is an outstanding feature of present-day life. The effect of course varies; in an extreme case, sexual development may be stopped and the achievement of maturity prevented entirely; in a milder case, a man may merely show an exaggerated devotion to his mother.

A severe but classical difficulty of this sort was demonstrated by a man who did not seek treatment until his early thirties. His reasons for doing so then were not at all connected with his obviously deranged sexual life. As soon as he discovered that in reality all his problems centered around his extreme attachment to and dependence upon his mother, he refused to continue treatment, unconsciously choosing to remain a child all his life.

The father in the family, who must face up to the new situation too, often finds it difficult for reasons similar to those which apply to the mother. His effectiveness at this period will be exactly proportionate to what it has been throughout childhood. There is no greater nonsense abroad than the notion that the father can take it easy until the children become adolescent and then suddenly make his entrance as an imposing and acceptable authority. Unless he has already established a sound relation with his children, he will not do so now and will have to make his way through this period of stress as a bystander, no matter how much he blusters or "lays down the law." He may exhibit extreme opposition, particularly to his daughter's maturing, and be only antagonistic toward her attempts to free herself from her family. He was as much her first love as the mother was her son's, and he too has the same desire for his children's love. Underneath this is a strong wish to preserve his daughter's innocence and her sexual purity. This may exhibit itself in any degree, from real paternal protectiveness to frantic, irrational opposition to any boy who pays her attention. The results are no better than in the corresponding situation with the mother; the girl is only forced to fight the harder for her independence. In doing so she may be driven to behavior that will have unhappy consequences and that might have been avoided by a more permissive attitude on the part of the father.

He also has a prominent part to play in helping his son to comfortable maturity. If their earlier relationship has been one of strong mutual affection, the father will now be an indispensable guide and counselor for the boy. But where it has not, the relationship between the two is likely to be very flimsy and even destructive. A boy of seventeen came for help because he was having such miserable difficulties in school. He was known to be a talented youngster, but he was the despair of his teacher. He was a brilliant athlete but generally succeeded in keeping himself disqualified for athletic contests by the abysmal nature of his grades. His relations with his teachers were correspondingly unhappy. His story was not too unusual. From the boy's earliest days his father had been aloof and stern, always making demands and, it seemed to the boy, never giving affection and understanding. He had responded during his early years with a good deal of rebellion and misbehavior but never to a degree to warrant real concern. With his adolescent days he found himself powerful enough to return in full measure all the disappointment his father had caused him. It does not matter that in so doing the youngster often deprives himself of his dearest wishes, so long as the offending parent is punished. In this respect our lad was brilliantly successful.

The fact that we have laid some stress on the difficulties that beset the family at this time does not mean that there are not as many delights. In a large number of families the entire adolescent period is one in which there are happily only a few hazards to negotiate. But in every family there will be some signs, however slight, of the operation of the forces that we have talked about. The way in which parents approach the situation will determine how comfortable or strenuous it will all be. What, then, should the approach be?

The first rule that needs to be emphasized is that there is nothing to be frightened about. The pages of today's newspapers, with their unceasing recitation of adolescent disaster, are enough to frighten the most hardy and self-assured. But these are the exceptions; newspapers do not print stories of the day-by-day lives of comfortable families. The whole process of adolescence is one of growth, just as everything before it has been. It is only more violent, more tumultuous and more exciting. But it is growth nevertheless and it is natural. The acceptance of it *as* that will be the greatest possible support to the whole situation.

Nevertheless, even when this is understood, there are many practical matters to be dealt with. Parents ask, "Shall we continue to exercise control as we have done? Shall we make the decisions and see to it that they are lived up to? Shall we let the youngster decide and keep out of it?" Parents must remember that they are still parents even though the child is growing up. The worst thing they can do is to abdicate their roles and turn over the whole enterprise to the youngster. That is a kind of abandonment. Neither can they continue simply to impose regulations as they did when these adolescents were children.

The greatest struggle between parents and children is over the amount of freedom the boy or girl is to have in managing his own life. The rule is that he should have all the freedom he can actually support. This does not mean that he should have all the freedom he wants. In a group discussion, when asked to define what he meant by the freedom that he thought he should have, a seventeen-year-old said, "Well, for me freedom is the right to do whatever I want to do whenever I want to do it." He had no sooner said it than he realized the absurdity of it. But he was right; that is the definition of freedom to many an adolescent. And that is something no one can have. The child may and probably will demand liberties which he can by no means handle, and which will lead him into all sorts of difficulties. How can the parent judge what freedoms the child is able to manage? That is an individual matter and no hard and fast rule can be given. The child's total reaction must be taken into account. If he is inclined to act on impulse and without thinking, if he is easily led into any kind of undertaking that others may propose, then he is clearly in need of closer guidance than the more thoughtful child. A youngster who is irresponsible in most of his everyday activities is liable to be irresponsible wherever you meet him. It is reasonable for the parents to see to it that the young person meet the fundamental requirements made of him before they relinquish their right to exercise a restraining hand.

The way in which supervision is exercised is perhaps as important as that it be exercised. There is general agreement that the youngster of this age finds it much easier to accept parental decisions (even if the decisions go against the youngster's wishes) when the parents have attempted to discuss the situation with him in a reasonable way. The youngster then feels that he has a chance to express himself, has had his day in court and has been treated as a responsible human being. "That's all very fine," many a parent has said, "but what is one to do if, even after open discussion, the child stubbornly sticks to his own point of view and refuses to be convinced?" If the matter is extremely hazardous or serious and the parents are sincerely and strongly opposed, the final decision must be in their hands. But they cannot expect youngsters to accept and to comply with decisions which are capricious, unreasonable or taken for parental convenience. The parent who has no considered policy and who judges every situation on the spur of the moment is liable to be in trouble. If a request to go out, for example, is refused at one time and granted at another, for no apparent reason, the youngster is going to take the view that any refusal can probably be obviated. If, however, there is an agreed-upon policy which is subject at all times to review and change as the circumstances warrant, the youngster has something solid to count on.

It would be a wise plan at the beginning of each school year to call a family council in which the matters of the coming year were discussed and general plans decided upon. At this time the youngsters could, with their parents, come to reasonable decisions about matters of privilege and responsibility. Nights out, hours, entertainment in the home, budget restrictions and allowances, home responsibilities and expectations, school requirements could all be settled at this time. In this way there is understanding on the part of both the youngster and his parents and a harmonious working arrangement can be reached.

But when all possible rules of thumb have been laid down and every case covered, the one great fundamental requirement is that the parents shall understand the processes going on in the youngster and their own parts in the drama.

If they do, and if they are prepared to accept inevitable changes, they will find their problems of adjustment easier. They cannot afford to relinquish family management or family life to the uncertainties of the inexperienced youngster. Nor can they afford to insist upon the unquestioned superiority and finality of their own judgments and decisions. The day for control by edict is over. Parents must recognize that their usefulness and their authority will now rest upon their own validity as parents and not upon their fast diminishing powers. Blustering, threatening and denial will fail to work now—if they ever worked at all. The old formulas of "as long as you live in this house" or "as long as you are under my roof" or "while I control the purse string," etc. are challenges which the adolescent can rarely fail to take up. Nor will understanding parents wish to challenge. On the contrary, they will want for their youngsters the surest and fullest maturity that can be had. If this wish is clear, their judgments will be tempered by it. And they will offer as much freedom as the youngster's powers will warrant and as much strength from themselves as is needed to give real support.

Inevitably, parents will have to be the last court of appeal and must stand ready to protect the young from their own not infrequent impulses toward excess and indiscretion. But the necessity will be rarer where the youngster feels that his approaching maturity is welcomed by his parents, that they stand ready to help him in every way to achieve it, yet will furnish as before strong and reliable support in situations that threaten to overwhelm him.

For themselves, parents will look for a continuation of the old happiness in parent-child relations. But with a very great difference. For with this period in life the process of enrichment and enlightenment can begin to go in both directions, from child to parent as well as from parent to child. The inquiring mind and roving curiosity, the intellectual robustness and creative energy of the adolescent can vitalize the whole of family life. Where parents know their own position and recognize their youngster's needs as acceptable, where the realities of the changing parent-child relationship are served, the experience of these years should be happy and profitable for both.

VI

The Adolescent and His Friends

Man is a social animal. It is an indispensable part of every individual's life to find associations and relationships on which he can rely. This gives him his group, his place of belonging. At first his associations are confined to the family group itself, within which he gradually acquires the ability to give and take. Very young children, from eighteen months to three or four years, have only a rather tenuous connection with the other children with whom they are brought together in play. During this time they are simply learning the rudiments of how to form a real friendship. Over the years, through a gradual testing and retesting process, stronger ties are formed and the basis is laid for durable and satisfying later relationships.

School life brings widening associations and the formation of the first ties of friendship outside the family group. These early ties, however, will not withstand any great pressure from the outside, nor will these loyalties be proof against the greater loyalties to home and family. However, with every passing year the child's focus is more outward and his independence of family support and control constantly increases. More and more he shows an ability to attach himself to others and to find and try new ways of feeling, doing and thinking—always with the underlying family attachments unimpaired. It is during this time (the period from seven to twelve), for example, that gang formation has its beginnings. These "gangs" are only pale reflections of the later, much stronger, group alliances of adolescence. Nevertheless, they have the same basic structure—the elements of inclusion and exclusion and of lip service, at least, to the idea of deathless loyalty.

During this period both boys and girls are getting to the point where they will be ready to join such associations as the Boy and Girl Scouts, which place much reliance upon the child's ability to form group allegiance and to work and play in the team. Adult supervision and help is required to make this undertaking successful and the youngsters as a whole still show great dependence on the adult leader. Quite apart from such formal organizations, however, are the independent groupings that children of this age will make on their own. These are the clubs and societies with which anyone who has had the privilege of doing much work with such young children is familiar. Though they appear at first to be quite binding and durable, they all have certain noticeable characteristics that reveal the fact that their durability is only apparent. There is a great deal of strife and tension. Today's deathless bond is repudiated tomorrow. Both the membership and the leadership are constantly changing: the youngster most admired and sought after on Tuesday will have withdrawn from the group under pressure on Thursday, to be succeeded by a replacement. There is constant striving for position and dominance. These things are all evidence that the problems of actual co-operation are still not solved and that the group does not have any real solidarity.

With adolescence outside attachments become stronger and more varied. They fall into three easily identifiable categories, each having its own characteristics and motivation: 1) attachments to associates of the same sex, individually and in groups; 2) attachments to adults of the same or opposite sex, other than parent; 3) attachments to the opposite sex. Only 1) and 2) will be considered in this chapter, since the association with the opposite sex is of such importance that it must be dealt with separately.

There is at this age a discernible sharpening of sexual differences. The boy is becoming a man and the girl a woman, and as they are drawn together they are also separated. This separation is accompanied by a strengthening of the ties of each to his own kind. Here lies the basis for the formation of real and durable friendships between members of the same sex. These friendships are strongly colored by the over-all peculiarities of adolescent emotional life—intensity, variability and exaggeration. Two youngsters of this age often give the appearance of being mutually absolutely dependent. They play together, work together and would live together if circumstances allowed them to. At times they may seem to be almost one and the same person, the lines between them are so fuzzy and indefinite. They wear each other's clothes, exchange possessions in a casual way, talk in the same manner with the same inflections. Not infrequently they go to such extremes in their indiscriminate exchange that when one meets one of them, he or she is scarcely recognizable because of being dressed entirely in the other's clothes.

Communication at this time is a primary necessity. Apparently they have no assurance that a relationship can endure unless it is constantly bolstered up by the exchange of ideas and experiences. Often two youngsters who have only a half-hour ago left each other at the front door will find it necessary to talk on the telephone for as much as an hour. Any idea that the subjects discussed could have been settled in less costly ways is completely irrelevant, as any parent will discover who makes the attempt to interfere. Some youngsters appear to find it difficult to be separated even to sleep, often doing their homework together after school and then spending the best part of the evening on the telephone comparing results and discussing the endlessly fascinating affairs of their existence. The minutiae of school associations, the offenses of the oppressive teachers, the insufferableness of whoever at the moment is the despised and abhorred, the charms or loathesomeness of some boy or girl, the burdens of life under adult jurisdiction, coming excitements and past suffering, all must be extensively reviewed.

Much about these relationships has at least the air of secrecy. Telephone conversations are preferably conducted behind closed doors. In each other's homes conversation is always in private. Any idea the adult has that inquiry will bring satisfaction is likely to be false. Usually the answer is, "Oh, we can't tell you. This is something private."

In large part, this communication and secretiveness is a matter of imitation designed to orient the youngster to the group with which he is associating himself. He is forming tastes that are independent of his family's. Many times there is an absolute slavishness about his identifications and imitations. Whatever his current group has set up as standards of speech, dress, interests, posture, attachment or detestation will be passionately adhered to. All this produces the stereotyped adolescent with the unmistakable stigmata. The sweater five or six times larger than necessary, the socks, the saddle shoes or loafers, the movie hero, the pin-up girl, the autographed raincoat, the charm bracelets, the long lank hair lapping over one eye, the crew cut, the slang, the bubble gum, the soda fountain stool, the Saturday movie—they are all marks of group solidarity; they bolster the sense of belonging.

Individual associations by easy stages enlarge to form groups and cliques. As I pointed out in an earlier chapter, these normal and inevitable groupings should not be confused with the so-called delinquent "gangs" of the big city, which are a danger and challenge to society as a whole. The average adolescent group has a healthy basis, for it arises out of the need of the young person to find a place in the world where he belongs and is accepted by others whose interests, capacities and attitudes are like his own. It gives him an opportunity for self-expression, affords an arena for his activities, and a testing ground for his ideas and convictions. More than this, the adolescent derives a deep emotional satisfaction from the circumstances of group life. Groups exist both by inclusion and exclusion. The group to which one belongs is one's "in-group." Everyone outside of it belongs to an "out-group." The inclusiveness of belonging gives one strength through solidarity, and the acceptance that belonging implies bolsters one's self-esteem. There is a rigid hierarchy for such groups, from most desirable to most undesirable. Obviously the effort is to be accepted by the most desirable.

Least exclusive perhaps are the "clubs." Every high school now has "interest clubs" or "hobby clubs." Here common interests guide the youngsters' choice of associates: sewing, stamp collecting, dramatics, dancing, poetry, journalism or any one of the now multifarious activities of the youngster. Boy Scouts and Girl Scouts, Y.W.'s and Y.M.'s offer a similar outlet for legitimate interests and associations.

Inside the larger juvenile community are numerous smaller and less formal groups—little more than cliques composed of kindred spirits who cling together for the purpose of protection and self-advancement. In the fraternity and sorority of high school and college years we find the ultimate outcropping of this tendency. Here the expression of exclusiveness has reached the saturation point. The real value of the fraternity is that it keeps people out. Thus those who are "in" gain importance. Parenthetically, let the reader beware before taking the amused view that these are the quaint customs of adolescents only. They are the "quaint customs" of the adult world too. What else is the country club, the club of any sort, but an adult expression of a tendency first seen in adolescence?

Naturally, the glory of the club depends upon the status of its members. Nowhere than among adolescents is there a greater tendency to idealize the individual of prominence and achievement. Every fraternity wants the football hero and every sorority the corresponding girl. To associate with one who is much sought after is to shine in reflected glory. For the youngster who is all too unsure of his own values and importance this is a vital concern. The question of who is valuable and important varies. Sometimes it is decided by the endowments of the youngster, which make him a natural leader. The talented boy or girl will have a considerable claim on the attention of his associates. But, it is noticeable at this age that the student who is most outstanding academically will rarely enjoy the same prestige as the athlete who has difficulty in keeping up to scratch. Sometimes among adolescents as among their elders material power confers value on the individual. Clothes and automobiles, for instance, may give their possessor a worth that has no relation to his real qualities. Similarly the youngster who is cocksure, a braggart, apparently daring and disdainful of adult authority, acquires a certain glamour. Whatever and however prestige is attained, it is an intangible quality that makes the youngster desirable and sought after and the nucleus of a group.

It is axiomatic that "children are cruel." So too are adolescents. Everyone is familiar with the difficulties and obstacles they can put in the way of a newcomer. At his approach, all differences within the group are set aside and a solid front of rejection presented toward the outsider. A good deal of the misery and heartache of youngsters during the school life arises out of this fact of exclusion. Their infinite longing for acceptance, and their inability to rely wholly on themselves, make approval in the form of admission to a group the indispensable ingredient of happiness. To be left out, to be disregarded or passed over, is misery indeed. Seldom do these young people reject each other in ways that are subtle or that soften the blow. Preferably they do it by the sledge-hammer method. You are not simply not in, you are out. This kind of sadistic unconcern is not simply a group quality. Individually these youngsters are often capable of immeasurable cruelty to each other. By gossip and innuendo, by lampooning and ridicule, they turn upon each other with what at times seems like savagery. Each knows only too well the other's weakness, for it is his own. This produces the lonely sufferer, the defiant lone wolf, driven out of the crowd and hiding his injuries under whatever disguise comes easiest to him. Some youngsters show their hurt easily and openly and can be helped to weather it. Others conceal it or deny it it by transparent devices. There are always those who turn away from the unfriendly environment and withdraw into themselves, repudiating the group. Some become hostile and revengeful.

In the ordinary course of events these problems are solved as the child matures. He finally finds his place. For the average child this is relatively easy; for the child who is off the beaten track or in some way unusual it is bound to be more difficult. Not unless the problem gets very acute and really threatens to disrupt the youngster's life is he apt to need psychiatric help. Sometimes, however, his misery is so obvious and so destructive that help is sought. This was true of Tom, who was about to be asked to leave his fourth school. He was not stupid; all his teachers recognized his superior abilities. Nevertheless, he did badly and was the despair of those who were trying to instruct him, a fact that apparently failed to disturb him in the least. It was always noticed, but rather casually, that Tom never seemed to be part of the group, rarely participated in school activities, and was generally unpopular. His unpopularity was ascribed by those who knew him to his bitter and cynical attitude. He accepted nothing and cared for nothing, was loyal to nothing and harshly sarcastic and critical of his associates. His interests appeared to be wholly intellectual and he seemed to have no wish to be accepted by any part of the group.

Tom's indifference was only apparent. When he began to talk about his troubles he was not very far from tears. The cynical covering disappeared and, underneath, it was easy to see the tormented quivering child whose disappointed longings for love had driven him to take refuge behind a mask of hate. And small wonder. Tom had lost his mother after his third brother was born. He was then eight, and already beginning to feel rejected and undesirable because attention had been deflected from him to his younger brothers. His father, an intellectual, preoccupied man, had little time for his children even though he loved them deeply. Only when they sought him out was he able to give them adequate paternal attention. For Tom this had never been possible, and he had turned to his mother instead. She had been his stand-by, and with her loss his world fell apart. His stepmother was not much help. With the best will in the world, she could not "get at" this passionately loyal little boy who refused to give the love that had been his mother's to an intruder. Soon, too soon, his alienation and the discomfort it caused in the family brought the solution of boarding school. This was the climax for Tom. Assailed by the conviction that he was unloved and unwanted, he was wholly unable to cope with the new environment. And so his defense.

He did not dare expose himself to any more hurts. The bare possibility of further rejection was more than he could endure to contemplate. If he was worthless and an outcast, very well, he would live as one. Furthermore, his behavior was an effective punishment of those who had injured him. Resenting his father for remarrying and for having always found his brothers more acceptable than himself, he was deeply determined to retaliate by causing him equal disappointment. To his father, proper achievement and compliance were important. Nothing was more humiliating to him than to have this eldest son a failure. And Tom knew it. By the time he was brought for help he was deeply enmeshed in this destructive program and was unable to stop it himself.

The needs of the adolescent are many but they can all be summarized under security. This is central and in a large way includes almost everything else. His security will rest in a satisfactory answer to his needs for love. In the last analysis that must be found in the discovery of a compatible partner and finally in marriage and children. He must also find satisfaction for his needs for achievement, accomplishment, position, and prestige. Achievement is tied to life occupation with its material rewards. The search for a settled vocation is an important part of the effort of this time of life. Position and prestige are of course related to and derived from vocation and accomplishment, but they have an importance in themselves which warrants giving them particular consideration. The dictionary (*The Shorter Oxford English Dictionary*) calls prestige "an illusion; a conjuring trick; a deception, an imposture"; and derivative of this meaning, "glamour; influence or reputation derived from previous character, achievements, or success." Illusion or not, it constitutes a large part of every person's motivation. It finally comes down to a real or imagined ascendancy which arouses envy and rivalry in others. It may depend upon material position, of which the classic symbol, we will say, is the possession of a mink coat—or an automobile, or a home in a fashionable district, or jewels, or a rich grandfather, or political position. It may also rest upon more solid virtues such as high achievement in academic, scientific or artistic fields. It may depend upon character traits which are presumed to be intrinsically valuable, though perhaps it should be said that this is a far more infrequent basis for prestige than once it was or than we should like to see it. Finally, unusual accomplishment of any kind often lends a prestige.

No group is more susceptible to the need for status and prestige than are the adolescents. Unsure of themselves and their own values, requiring above all things the approval and acceptance of those around them, they are always urgently seeking ways of finding these things. Very early in their life they wanted the admiration and approval of their parents. Now it is the admiration and approval of their associates which they seek, for it is among them that they expect to find the answer to their needs for love. The less secure a youngster is, the more slavishly will he imitate his successful contemporaries. But whatever their state of mind, they must, to some extent, comply with the demands of those around them. It would be unfair to interpret their apparent complaisance as evidence that they are entirely without any allegiance to fundamental principles and values or can be completely seduced by conjuring tricks. On the contrary, they are motivated by the most idealistic considerations and long for a life governed by them. But they want love and acceptance too.

So it comes about that they are often the center of an unhappy conflict. The easy, the glittering, and the sensational seem to achieve more quickly the fundamental position which they envy. As they emerge into this new awareness, they can quickly see how far the practices of the world, and the values to which it gives real allegiance, differ from those to which they have been reared and to which the world gives lip service. It does not take them long to discover that the honest virtues taught in most homes often do not appear to bring the same rewards as more dubious but more spectacular practices do. Their deep yearnings for attachment to an ideal are constantly assaulted by their need for a sense of position and belonging. The youngster feels that he must be popular. It is more desirable than anything else. To be so it would seem wise to emulate those who are. And right there the fat is in the fire. For what if those who are popular also—as too often happens—fail to exemplify the kind of character traits which are desirable and admirable?

For the youngster, this state of affairs often results in a frequent shift of allegiance. First one and then another person will attract, and be discarded. A new group may be approached with high hopes and then, because of some painful experience, have to be repudiated. Another one will be chosen, perhaps for reasons which seem to the concerned adults very dubious. This is the point at which the problem of "bad companions" often looms large. The solid youngster who has a good hold on himself and his values is not likely to be bewitched and enchanted by bad associates, but the unsure and the uncertain, those with feelings of insufficiency, may very easily be carried along by any youngster or group of youngsters who seem to have a grasp on the desirable things of life.

This was true of Josie, a youngster in her very early teens who was the despair of her parents because of her incorrigible determination to associate with youngsters considerably older than herself and of very unsavory reputation. Her parents regarded her as unmanageable. And it was a fact that no matter what they said or did Josie continued to pursue her own course. She was utterly unreliable and entirely beyond any counsel or persuasion. Punishment was least effective. She was beginning to develop a great deal of interest in what boys thought of her, and was susceptible to almost any kind of influence. Her manner of dress, her hair style, her smallest mannerism, her behavior in every particular, were all dictated by "what the other girls are doing" or what she imagined they were doing. The difficulty was that this youngster could be counted upon to follow the request of any boy who paid her the slightest attention.

This was a situation obviously made for trouble. The young boys, who were not themselves too well established, promptly began to take advantage of her easy compliance. The rest of the story can easily be imagined.

Fortunately, her parents were able to bring her for treatment before she became too deeply involved. The explanation of her behavior lay in the fact that she had, through her upbringing, acquired such a deep sense of her own unworthiness and unlovableness that she was eager to do anything to assure to herself enough love and attention. This need was so overpowering that she was unable to exercise any judgment about her actions. Her teachers and her associates, as well as her parents, were completely bewildered by her outrageous behavior and only those who were anxious to express their power by influencing her were gratified. Her story is so commonplace that it seems well to quote it here, for very often, where it would be neither expected nor recognized, such problems are found to have their real focus in the family.

As a rule, adolescent friendships follow a comfortable course and will only rarely require psychiatric attention. Nevertheless, even in the normal way, situations may arise that are serious enough to call for vigorous action. A really harmful associate may be idealized, for the incorrigible, seemingly daring and brilliantly defiant youngster is often a natural leader and influences all those around him. The adolescent can't be challenged too much. Any activity which does that is apt to get his immediate and enthusiastic support. Dare him, and he'll do anything. Or a group with known unhealthy tendencies may win the youngster's allegiance. His sense of loyalty may hold him to a false and dangerous cause, and he may insist on a course which the parents are sure is going to bring him to grief. What then is the parent to do?

It had better be stated quickly that the job is liable to be a hard one. It will take the greatest delicacy to interfere effectively or to change the situation. The first and strongest tool parents can have is a determination to be fair and reasonable, and to expect the same attitude of their boys and girls. Any issuing of edicts, any business of announcing, "We don't approve of him (or her or them) and that's the end of it," is foolish and unreasonable. Sit down with the youngster; present to him quietly but firmly the facts as they are known; point out the dangers and the possible difficulties. Very often he will be persuaded by the justice of the parents' position. "This group," the parents know, "is made up of a lot of unhappy and disturbed young people." There has to be concrete evidence. No generalizations about just not liking the "look of the thing." The youngster's rejoinder will be, "What's wrong, he's a nice guy and a friend of mine." It isn't enough that parents simply don't like the friend in question or the club or the gang. They must take the trouble really to find out. Perhaps on second thought or better acquaintance, they will understand the reason for their child's allegiance and will be less anxious to interfere. Or, it may all look worse, and they may discover that the situation is one that definitely has to be interfered with. Obviously, the best way to know is to have firsthand close acquaintance with the child's friends. The doubtful associate, the questionable crowd should be brought to the home and the whole setup examined there. Any attempt to make a judgment from outside will only cause resentment.

Not until the whole situation has been examined and a decision reached, should one tackle the problem with the youngster. If the parents are sure of their ground and confident that they have given the question fair objective consideration, there is much less danger of frayed tempers or autocratic verdicts. Reason will usually do the job. If the child can be shown that his friends are definitely not desirable, and that he is likely to come to grief if he continues to

associate with them, he is apt to agree to give up the unhappy alliance. If reasoning fails, along with persuasion and
urging, more stringent ways will probably have to be tried.
This is where trouble begins. The adolescent hates above all
to be ordered about. He is pressing for his own right to decide. Parents may let themselves get angry or exasperated
with the seeming stubborn blindness of the young. The session which was planned as a reasonable discussion may degenerate into a name-calling brawl, and all is lost. If the
parents really believe on good evidence that a given association must be stopped, and they are reduced to the exercise
of authority, they certainly can't give up and run away from
it. But they will be smart to go at it with a light hand.
They can make it clear that they don't like the kind of thing
they are having to do (and they shouldn't like it), but that
they would be negligent if they didn't do it anyway. They
had better not waver, even while minimizing the nature of
their disciplinary action. They ought to have a right to get
from the youngster an admission that they are trying to act
in good faith and to do what they really feel is necessary,
and not simply throwing their weight around. Once they
have made a decision, they must see that it is carried out.

Sometimes, if the matter is arousing a lot of feeling in the
youngster, it may be a good idea to agree to let someone
else make the final decision—someone whom the youngster
trusts and respects. With the odium of parental heavyhanded-
ness removed, the youngster will have less ground for objection. Arbitration is a good practice in any dispute, and no less
in situations like these. When the issue isn't open-and-shut,
discussion may clarify it for everyone and the youngster's
wish perhaps permitted to stand. It isn't a poor idea to give
everyone the benefit of the doubt, but it must be done whole-
heartedly, not grudgingly. Watchful waiting will prove
whether or not the right stand has been taken.

Whatever is done, it is important for parents to know their

children's friends as well as they can. They should try to accept them openheartedly, even if they can't see what on earth the attraction is. Maybe they will find out. If it is a good and understandable connection, they will be glad they didn't leap before they looked; and if it is a bad one, they will be glad they waited until they were absolutely sure of their ground. Above all, their children's confidence in them will be kept intact and the door between them still open for communication. That is worth anything. For there will in all probability be occasions when the youngster's wishes have to be overruled, and he can accept this if his relations with his parents have made him sure of their love and fairness. He will then be willing to accept the strength of the parents as something to lean on and not something to fight against. He may not show it at the time the unwelcome decision is reached, but he will later if the rules have been followed. In the shortest terms these rules are:

1. Don't expect your youngsters to follow your own likes and dislikes so far as people are concerned.
2. Respect their right to make their own choices as far as possible.
3. Know their friends by making them your friends.
4. Reserve your judgments until you are absolutely sure you are right and have evidence of it.
5. Talk things over with the youngster reasonably, objectively and without prejudice, and listen to their opinions, which are valuable.
6. If, after all this, you still feel that you must interfere with some association of theirs, give your reasons and be sure to make it clear that you are interfering because you are certain that it is necessary for the youngster's welfare.
7. Having made a decision, stick to it, and see that it is

carried out. Flabbiness and indolence won't earn the respect of these teen-agers.

8. Always, all the time, keep the door open for discussion and communication.

These rules are tough to follow but they will work. Parents who have built a relationship with their children which makes this procedure natural won't have any trouble anyway.

It is not only with their contemporaries but with the adults around them that youngsters of this age establish relationships. Teachers, counselors, ministers, group leaders or friends of the parents particularly may occupy an important position. All of them, of course, are obvious parent substitutes to whom, as such, the youngster can turn with confidence in their guidance, help, and friendship. Teachers especially are apt to be cast in this role; and a devoted and inspiring teacher provides an ideal that proves an invaluable steadying influence during a difficult time. Parents are sometimes made unhappy and jealous by this tendency of their youngsters to turn to other adults with their confidences and their needs. They will, then, do anything they can to break up what they induce themselves to believe is an unfortunate relationship. Why can't the child turn to the parent? If the reader remembers what has been pointed out about the child's need to find various kinds of images to imitate and with whom to identify, so to discover his own personality, the answer is easy. The new adult, representing a different point of view and different attitudes, provides the child with another ideal to test out. There may be many such enthusiasms in the child's life and many incidences of the hero worship which naturally ensues when an adult seems to the child to contain all the virtues that he himself wishes to have. Every encouragement should be given to the youngster to follow these ideals. Unless the chosen adult is a pernicious influence, it is a happy event. The youngster who

hero-worships openly is one who is sure of parental tolerance and love. He has no fear that his parents will oppose
his new association or feel themselves threatened by his
expanding interests. For the parents there will be some risk
in opposing it, for the child will sense their jealousy or their
wish to hold on to him. If he yields, he will be retarded in
his drive toward maturity; if he stands on his convictions,
the parents' hostility will create a gulf between them.

In all they do, young people are sometimes going to veer
away from the family, its attitudes and points of view. Most
parents, probably, are upset when their youngsters are
drawn toward people and groups which are alien. "We never
had such ways." "The girl is perfectly nice, but she is Jewish
or Catholic, or not Jewish or not Catholic, or foreign or
hasn't any background, and I can't imagine why she wants
to go with such people." As parents, we would all like to
see our own convictions, tastes and attitudes validated by
the young. We are inclined to the belief that our own views
are the best and we don't want that belief attacked. It
is much less challenging to have Joe and Jane grow up
to believe in the unquestioned rightness of the Republican
(or Democratic) party, private enterprise, as Papa defines
it (or its opposite), Smith and Yale, the Presbyterian (or
any other) church, sterling silver, naming sons for fathers
and/or daughters for mothers, belonging to the Book-of-
the-Month Club as the touchstone of "culture," living at
home, and other such sound ideas, than it is to have them
running after false gods. They may turn up as horrid little
leftists who bite the hands that are feeding them (or stick-
in-the-mud conservatives). It is likely to be distressing when
the young scion of the house decides that he would rather
be a carpenter than go into father's good sound firm. Or
perhaps a daughter will do some hideous thing like marrying the "wrong boy," or maybe not marrying at all but being
suspected of doing something much worse. There just isn't

any way of talking to these young people who insist that they prefer good old comics to any book or even perhaps prefer any old book not recommended by the dear old Book-of-the-Month Club. And as for religion, that doesn't bear thinking about. Not that father and mother have been to church since Aunt Ethel's funeral, but it is just as well to go on thinking what you have always thought and not be disturbed by the young.

The trouble with this fantasy is that it isn't apt to come off unless you have reared a rubber stamp, and parents may have some trouble doing that these days. But it isn't so bad as it looks. A good many of the errant will return to the fold, wanderings over and unfortunate alliances forgotten, and there will be a gratifying reconciliation to the ways of sense and wisdom. Sometimes, to be sure, such a pleasant rectification will not take place, and parents will have to face the fact that a youngster simply isn't going to do what's expected and grow up to follow in the traditional path. Perhaps he will select as an ideal someone and something far removed from the ideals of the family. If he does, he will be following the path of human development in its most exciting form—becoming an individual in his own right.

In all these years when the child is branching out into a wider world, finding new and different associates, identifying himself with first one and then another cause, the process of growth is going on. From complete dependence upon family and home, he is moving toward independence—and ultimately he will find himself in the enterprise.

VII

The Adolescent and the Wider Community

As development proceeds, the adolescent's interests expand over a wider and wider range and begin at last to comprehend the community in which he lives. As its influence is felt by the youngster, he in turn can begin to make himself felt in the community. However, he cannot take his place in that community as an effective member until he is adjudged by it to be sufficiently responsible to take care of himself and to avoid inflicting danger upon it.

Regulations about his entrance into community living are apparent. He may not vote until he is twenty-one, at which time he has been arbitrarily determined to be mature. The age at which he may marry is also set, though it varies in the different states. There seems to be a preponderance of opinion that when a boy is eighteen and a girl sixteen they are mature enough to decide to marry. On what this is based, beyond mythology, the author is not prepared to say. A couple of states permit marriage without parental consent between boys of fourteen and girls twelve, and at the other extreme, two states require the males to be twenty-one and the females eighteen before contracting marriage. Other regulations come easily to mind. Most states have a minimum age below which the youngster is required to attend school, the age at which automobiles may be operated is also under general regulation, and more and more the work-age is being set by law.

Whatever the restrictions and regulations, the underlying implication is that the community recognizes the now imminent entry of the young person into full participation. They further show the community concern that adolescents shall not be exploited (as in the regulation of working ages), deprived (as in the regulation of educational requirements), or allowed to undertake responsibilities for which they are felt not to be prepared (the regulation of the right to contract marriage).

The youngster, now physically mature with a mastery of his material environment, is eager for at least some part of adult privileges. Wanting to become an independent self-operating grown-up, he has a tendency to assert himself as independent of the family jurisdiction and judgment in anything and everything that concerns him. Many times there will be a demand to move away from the family in the physical sense, to travel, to "get away from home," and he may insist that his parents must make this possible.

The author calls to mind the case of a competent and quite independent youngster of sixteen who developed the notion that her parents could only be monstrous if they did not allow her to go to Europe on her own (except for the minor fact that they had to finance the trip). The parents were at first so taken aback that they allowed themselves to give a halfway assent. They soon realized, however, that the program was an unrealistic one for which the child was not prepared and from which she would not benefit. When they began to oppose her, she was extremely hostile and acted as if her parents wished to deprive her of every possible satisfaction in life. When, however, their own minds were made up and they took an extremely firm position, very reasonably but unalterably, the youngster was relieved and went along happily with the alternate plans that her parents offered her. She later admitted that she had been very much frightened at the prospect of carrying out her own program and really had only put up a fight for it because she feared that she would be showing weakness and cowardice if she didn't.

At about sixteen or seventeen the adolescent's blossoming concern with community problems and interests may lead him as a volunteer into some of the welfare activities of his community. Most schools encourage the youngster to consider the social problems of the world he lives in, to study them, to observe the operation of the agencies concerned with them and to participate in them so far as possible. Many schools encourage them to select some definite field of activity on which to focus their attention. Thus one school may adopt a family, another may choose to occupy itself with the problems of the local boys' club. One set of schools in New York, for instance, has elected to support an agency which concerns itself exclusively with the placement of infants for adoption. All such activity expresses the same thing —the widening and deepening of the youngster's interest as a near citizen in his community.

As the young person comes into contact with the outside world in all its various forms and with all its various defects and disappointments, he is apt to experience a considerable reaction. For, as we know, little in the world of action and reality and compromise bears much resemblance to what the child has grown up imagining it to be. He enters it with a background of fantasy and academic understanding. He is pretty much like the small boy who was disillusioned on a visit to Vermont to find "it doesn't look like Vermont. That was green on the map." What the young person has been familiar with is "the map." And that has been put together by adults who have decided, among other things, what it would be most desirable for the student to know.

How much resemblance is there between the textbook description of the operation of our democracy which every youngster hits in high school "Social Studies" and the way an ordinary political machine really works in an election district? Not very much. It can come as a decided shock to the young student to find out that someone has been shot at the polls because he wasn't obeying the orders of the ward boss. That wasn't mentioned in the discussion of the "electoral system" in his school course. No particular mention was made either of some of the more unsavory facts about the way in which this system of free government operates for minorities or for anyone who doesn't happen to suit the local management. What is a young person full of the most ardent ideals to think about a situation where everyone is created "equal" and where these "equals" find themselves living some in palaces and some in slums? Is he going to be favorably impressed by his discovery that in this land of "equal opportunity" some people can't find work and some must and do go hungry and without clothing or the decencies of life? And that some die for want of proper medical care? Not having learned to accept as yet the fact that the ideals we have set up for ourselves put a strain on the human character and are often lost or damaged by a mass of compromise or worse, he has been known to get angry and to flame with righteous indignation.

It is easy to understand why politics often interests youngsters of this age. Politics being the practical expression of the desire to regulate and manage the social order for the benefit of the population, the adolescent, with his known idealism, his eagerness for perfection, is bound to have his attention caught by it. But having had academic instruction in its goal of justice for all, he will not be long in discovering how far short politics falls of accomplishing its goal. The realization often hits him with a dull sickening thud. His questions will be: How can it happen? Why does it have to be that way? What makes people so much less than he has imagined them? This is "feet of clay" trouble with a vengeance, and he will seek answers and solutions in his own mind. Furthermore, he will want to try to translate his answers into actions. Not improbably, he will feel that the whole trouble lies with the adults who run the show. They have lost their ability to operate a proper system. Or the system they are operating is the wrong one and a new one must be found. What is more, he and his kind will be the ones to find it and remake the world nearer to the heart's desire.

By the most obvious steps the youngster is led to violent allegiances. This has been seen to happen time and again. Every demagogue knows how easily it can be done, and does it. Hitler did it, Mussolini did it, Stalin is doing it, we do it. No one who wishes to promote a cause is ignorant of the fact that nowhere can you get more intense and idealistic adherents than among the young. Their inexperience ensures that they will not be able to make cogent or careful judgments. All you have to do is promise them what you know they long for—Utopia—and they are for you. The difficulty is that these youngsters are infinitely exploitable. They throw their hearts and their energies at the feet of any savior, any leader, any Messiah. Never mind that he may change from day to day. During his ascendency each leader is supreme.

Then there is the question of jobs. There is no independence without economic independence. Many youngsters are insistent upon "going to work." This can, of course, apply only to three situations: after school hours, on holidays, after the termination of the school term. Some youngsters want to stop school in order to go to work, insisting that nothing matters except the opportunity to get into the work world and prove themselves. There are often grave conflicts between parents and children on this subject. The parents may well take the point of view that there is a long time in which work will be demanded and that the better the preparation, the more satisfaction and success the youngster will have in his work. They may suggest, plead, or command that he continue in school and not try to anticipate the work experience before he is ready for it or has anything to offer to the economic system. Then, of course, there is the youngster who is so terrified by the prospect of real adult life that he cannot endure the pressure of work even when it is clear that the time has come. If this is the case, the retardation will be observable in all phases of the youngster's life.

A young girl in this condition came to the author because she was openly unhappy and had developed some physical symptoms which were finally diagnosed as being of emotional origin. This youngster had been brought up in a broken home, with a mother and an aunt. Her only close relationship was with her aunt, and even that was marred by the fact that the aunt had other alliances which didn't permit her to give the girl all the love and devotion she needed. Nor, of course, had she had any kind of contact with a man as a father. From her early years, she had been given a great deal of freedom; in fact, she had been given hardly any supervision or guidance at all. Allowed to select her own schooling, she had, as a consequence, acquired almost none because she changed her mind so often. She had adopted and abandoned all sorts of vocations and had acquired no settled feeling about what she was or what she was doing. When she arrived at the point of having to enter the world outside her home, she was hopelessly at sea. All her fantasies and dreams were instantly destroyed, and she was unable to face her disillusionment.

All these reactions are consistent and harmonious with what we know about the adolescent. The difficulty is probably not in him so much as in his world, which does not provide the easy and gradual approach to maturity that an earlier world did. Where youngsters from their earliest years were observers of the adult world, carried along in it, taught its skills and attitudes, the transition was simple. The period of dependency was shorter. Much more was expected of the young child and the adolescent in a society largely dependent upon hand labor. The days of the kitchen stove, which demanded a full wood box, are far different from the present, where the stove not only requires no wood but is provided with so many gadgets that it can be left alone to prepare meals under the regulation of innumerable buttons. The child pouring milk from a bottle today has little in common with the boy of yesterday who, after watching his father milk, himself became a milker. Everything with which the child is surrounded—whether it be milk or shoes or suits or automobiles or any of an infinity of manufactured goods—appears from nowhere by a mysterious process wholly unknown to the child who receives them. It is a hard task indeed to give to today's city child a sense of the real source of his life needs. To them he can contribute nothing. The loom, the spindle, the smokehouse, the barn, the field, the orchard, the horse, the oxen, and all of the simple attributes of life a hundred years ago are gone. They will not be recovered unless the industrial machine is destroyed by its products.

Gone with those symbols of another age is the child's natural opportunity to be partially in the work world. Nowadays a youngster can scarcely know the meaning of work until he has completed a course of study designed to train him for a specific machine operation. Chores have not entirely disappeared from the domestic scene, but they are seldom insisted upon. Paper routes are with us, but they aren't what they used to be. Saturday work is becoming a thing of the past.

Yearly we see a crop of college graduates who have been told at the last minute by the commencement speaker that things are going to be tough, emerging into a world where there isn't any work worthy of their years of effort and finally settling down to operating elevators in the hope of "advancement." They don't like it. Someone has been giving them a poor steer. We have constructed and passed on a myth which does a great deal to injure and disillusion the young when they meet the story face to face. If we believed what we say about honest work well done, all would be well. But we don't believe it and, in fact, sometimes come perilously near to believing that dishonest work badly done but going unexposed is better than any other sort. No wonder then that many youngsters, when they get into this icy bath, think it a good idea to do nothing or as little as they can get away with, to turn in a shiftless account of themselves which will still let them hang on to the job, such as it is. Some of them would just as soon live on any sort of government largesse as try to push their way into the competitive world they see in front of them. They have, many of them, grown up with the idea that they are creative spirits of rare beauty and unless they can set up as artists or poets or actresses or some such glamorous people, they would prefer not to set up at all.

The economic state of affairs is clearly not altogether what it should be. That is admitted even by those most attached to the idea of "things as they are." Nor is any other aspect of the community into which the youngster will emerge as a functioning citizen. The problem of the parent is to discover how best to prepare the child for the adult realities —social, political, economic, sexual, and emotional—that he will inevitably meet. Specifically, how can the modern parent prepare his youngsters for the realities of socio-economic life without so disillusioning him that all effort becomes useless? Obviously full consideration must be given to reality. The fact that the world is as it is cannot be denied. The parents who try to deny it must be prepared to spare their young, through their own material power, the full force of reality, or to face the ire of those same young when they find out the facts. This may sound like a grim program. No one today imagines that the world is operating in a manner even re-

motely connected with the ideal. Everyone knows that we
are in the middle of political and social disaster. This knowledge must be introduced into the life of the child with
consideration for his ability to handle it and its impact upon
his sensitive organization. When all is said, there can be no
quarrel with the statement that children can stand the truth
better than they can stand any evasion of it or any effort
to sidestep its realities.

The wise parent will plan in advance. He will not exclude
the children from the realities of family life, especially the
realities of economic urgency. If it is true that the family
finances cannot cover what the child desires, then the child
must know it and be invited to participate in the family solution. One of the most deplorable and least effective ways of
dealing with the young is to "spare" him the knowledge of
the family situation. This can only result in a pouring out of
the family treasure upon him to the detriment of his own
sense of reality and the rights and privileges of the rest of the
family. This is a deception and one that will certainly come
home to roost. In the adult world in which he must make
his way, he is inevitably going to find out that he will be able
to have exactly what he can provide himself and no more.

To allow a child to grow up with the idea that he doesn't
have to work for his living is absurd. There are opportunities
all along the way for showing him that he does. Even in the
restricted, almost crippled home of today, there are chances
to make these facts real if the parent wants to. In spite of
the miracles of the washing machine, the stove, the vacuum
cleaner, there is work to be done, and much work if the
woman of the home is consulted. There is no reason for not
involving the youngest child in the realization that this work
has to be done. Parents must have the courage to see to it
that they exact enough from their growing children. As in
every other aspect of life, it is up to them. If they insist
upon sparing their children everything and trying to realize

their own dreams through their children, they should not be surprised if those same children decline all sense of responsibility and expect to receive gratis every sort of benefit. This is one way of excluding children from the home enterprise. They have a right to participate in it and to share in its work life. If they don't they will be far less well-prepared for the harsh realities which they must finally meet.

The same hard realities should be kept in mind in preparing the youngster for a vocation. Parents always hope that their children will exceed them in accomplishment and therefore in material rewards. The notion seems to be that the youngsters should expect to start where the parents left off. As often as not, this leads to a fantasy-like overvaluation of the child. Anything so mundane as self-preservation and self-support is not to concern him; he is to devote himself to "higher matters." The schools perpetuate this nonsense. The trend has been in the direction of deprecating any sort of real approach to the work world. Creative writing, for example, is now a part of every high school course, while many a harassed mother wonders if bed-making and housekeeping might not be in order as she remembers her days of dream glory when an "excellent" appeared on her paper on "The Place of Byron in the Romantic Movement" or her short story of the odyssey of a tortured young soul. However, junior and junior miss alike are given the idea that they are probably geniuses (the parental evaluation of themselves perhaps?) and far above the humdrum considerations which actuate the lesser ones, who have settled down to the mastery of some less glamorous activity such as good old plain typewriting or equally good old plain dressmaking. Time was, and until very recently, when no college girl was expected to make her bed or keep her own quarters clean. Presumably such utilitarian tasks would tarnish the bright glow of her intellect. Even the young gentlemen were carefully guarded from too much wrestling with practical details. Nowadays, the situation is more sensibly handled, since the availability of people to tend to the wants of the young ladies and gentlemen has diminished. It is reported that no great damage seems to be done them if they have to turn to and put in their share of time and effort on the practical aspects of living.

In the same way, any attempt to befuddle the issue and to refuse to face the fact that the political system under which we live is a man-made and very fallible one is liable to boomerang. Far better is it to share with these growing youngsters one's own concern over the dubious quality of what we do and how we do it than to try to present them with a fantasy which can only be an evasion or a falsification. To seek with them the answers which they require, to help them find their way toward the unhappily inescapable compromises of adult life, requires truthful facing of the issues. Nothing of the "you wouldn't understand this" school of thought is going to help. The fact is that the adolescent can understand if he is given any opportunity to. He can share in his parents' doubts and anxieties. The very fact of sharing means that he has someone from whom he can expect to get support and sympathy. How much better that he should be helped to arrive at his judgments by an accepting and open-minded attitude on the part of his parents than by the course of rebellion and denial.

There will inevitably be some differences of opinion between the parents and the adolescent children, who may believe that they should have liberty without restrictions, liberty of action and liberty of opinion. It will be the parents' task to harmonize the strivings of the youngster with the reality around him. Sometimes this will bring an outbreak of antagonism between the parents and the child. The child may feel that his judgment is mature enough to justify allowing him full range in all his activities. His parents will often doubt this and will very frequently be able to cite instances to prove their dire predictions of what will come to pass unless the youngster heeds them. They are often right and equally often wrong. The truth is that it is sometimes an act of abandonment to allow a youngster to take possession of all the privileges and powers that he asserts he wants. But it is an act of foolish restraint not to permit it when the child has proved himself capable, by steady advancement, of maintaining himself in situations requiring responsibility and judgment. As in everything else, each child is a law to himself and each child develops at a different rate. What is good for one will be impossible for another. But what is certainly true is that there must be a much more open mind about the business of gradual admission into the adult world.

VIII

Adolescent Sexual Behavior

This is the big troublesome question when the subject of the adolescent is introduced. Sometimes one gets the impression that the word adolescence is synonymous with the word sex. Certainly it is a problem of first-class importance, and, the author would surmise, one about which more people know less than about nearly anything else. An enormous amount of energy has been expended in trying to discover what the facts are. The questions that need answering are: What exactly is adolescent sexual behavior? Do adolescents have a recognizable pattern of sexual relations, and if so what is it? And the really big one: What is the desirable solution to this disturbing problem?

So far we haven't a definite answer to any of these questions. There isn't any Kinsey Report to give us the supposedly final word. Our sources of information are very often the public prints, in which any day we can discover that there has been an outbreak of sexual misbehavior among the young of some small or large town and that the "authorities" have put their heads together to find out what to do about it. Usually everyone has been locked up pending some decision. There are certain studies which undertake to tell us what college students have to say about themselves. Dorothy Dunbar Bromley collaborated on a study[1] in which college stu-

[1] *Youth and Sex, a Study of 1300 College Students*, by Dorothy Dunbar Bromley and Florence Haxton Britten. New York and London, Harper & Brothers, 1938.

dents, interviewed on this delicate topic, revealed that they were tolerant toward the idea of sexual relations during the college period outside of marriage. Dr. Clifford Adams of Pennsylvania State has stated[2] that it is safe to assume that 80 per cent of college students are having sexual relations. He bases his conclusions on a large number of past studies. There is no particular reason to quarrel with these figures.

When it comes to the high school age we are in less well-charted territory. The general attitude toward sexual experimentation at that age is one that would successfully prevent really finding out anything, for the whole idea of high school students' getting involved in sexual affairs is so disturbing that most people would prefer not to think about it. The powerful logic of assuming that what one doesn't talk about doesn't exist goes a long way to making people feel more comfortable. Largely we have to rely upon frequent scandalous reports and occasional "hideous revelations" which purport to expose the unspeakable goings-on of the high school young—the same young to whom many doubt the advisability of teaching the facts of reproduction and family life. Whatever the situation—and, admittedly, we know far too little about it—it is probably one that we would not enjoy if we were to know more.

However, there are certain things we do know about the pattern of behavior and inner workings of these youngsters which can guide us to some reasonable conclusions about how best to help them. We have already traced, in some detail, their sexual development as it shows itself during this period, and have noted their various solutions to the problem which their newly experienced sexual impulses pose. Briefly, there is at first a good deal of resistance and fear in the child himself. He hasn't the necessary courage to rush directly into sexual activity with others against the admoni-

[2] *How to Pick a Mate, the Guide to a Happy Marriage*, by Dr. Clifford R. Adams and Vance O. Packard. New York, E. P. Dutton & Co., Inc., 1946.

tions of his parents, society, and his own inner restraints. The pressure of his inner needs brings him to masturbation, but this, he feels, can only be a transitional and temporary solution, as well as a guilty one. No better is the interest in those of the same sex. Eventually the drive to grow, to find a permanent solution for his problem, pushes him into close association with the opposite sex. Social pressure, which grows steadily more intense, is another factor, for the youngster who does not show an interest in the opposite sex is sure to be suspect to his associates—though he may at times be envied for his apparent indifference and calm in the face of so vexing a situation.

The first sign of any formal sexual pattern in our society appears in the institution of "dating." The age at which dating begins varies enormously from class to class and from community to community. It is usually very tentative before fifteen, but after that age it is sure to become an established practice. They would be hardly parents indeed who would try to withstand the pressure beyond this age. The argument, "You are too young. There is plenty of time for that," will have lost its force, and the parents will not be able to stand up against the youngster's wails that everybody else has been doing it for a long time and that she will be doomed to horrible ostracism if she cannot do as others do. The problem of permitting or not permitting dating is largely confined to girls, since the feeling about boys dating is far less intense. Furthermore, the fact that girls are or are not permitted to date automatically controls the age at which boys begin.

What then is dating? It is a quite formalized institution of association between boys and girls. Since it involves both sexes, it is obviously sexual in its basic meanings. It is the first step of a long process which is designed to assure the discovery of a mate and, ultimately, marriage. But it is still a long way from marriage, and much must happen before the youngster even begins to consider anything so serious as that. A good many parents worry about dating because they misunderstand its meaning to the youngsters. They fear that this unsupervised and uncontrolled activity between boys and girls will lead to the frankly sexual and that in this there is danger. The fact appears to be that dating has no such goal. At first, and for some time, it does not include or assume any real sexual activity. In this sense it is far less emphatic than bundling, the ancient predecessor of petting. It is much more a "getting together" of boys and girls, usually in groups, for recreational and social purposes. The proper formula requires that the boy ask the girl for a date. This however does not signify that he has any intention of going on a twosome or will expect any sexual closeness. Once the preliminaries have been accomplished, there is a general relaxation and everybody can proceed to the business of having fun, however that may be defined in the particular group involved. There is more often than not a general fusion of dates. The group activities may be roller skating, ice skating, bowling, soda fountain sitting, listening to victrola records, dancing, going to concerts or merely sitting around exercising the mind by attempting the most popular of all sports—settling the world's problems.

Usually, in the beginning, dating is of the most mild and innocent sort, involving no grave difficulties about late hours and prolonged sessions. That comes later. The youngsters are usually satisfied with the excitement and delight of being on a date and for some time want nothing more. But a date they do want. Parents will often wonder why their children cannot pursue the same activities in the family circle or, if with a group of youngsters, at least at home where a mild parental eye can be kept upon the proceedings. There may be a good deal of dispute about this aspect of the situation. Children are informed that their parents are at a loss to know why they have to go out, or what on earth they do, or what is so fascinating about it, or why they can't have just as much fun here. This is obviously missing the point. It is the formal expression of the situation that is valuable.

One must understand the emotions involved here. What does dating mean to the youngster? For the girl, this is the first real evidence that a boy finds her desirable, that he accepts her as a girl rather than simply as a playmate. It is a gesture of choosing and to be thus chosen is the first of many crowns that she expects to wear. Anguish is the portion of the young girl who does not have a "date" on a Saturday when all her friends are known to be selected and approved of. There should be no misunderstanding that this is genuine suffering and represents real failure and rejection for the youngster involved. As for the boy, his first timid attempts to find recognition as a boy in a sexual sense are in these early moments. Dating may seem to be a simpler matter for him because his is the privilege of choosing. But the privilege of choice does not carry with it assurance of acceptance; the maiden has a choice in the matter, too. He suffers as much as she, if not more, when his advances are turned down. Sometimes it is harder to be openly rejected than merely to be passed by.

This can be a time of infinite woe and violent swings of mood, depending upon the success and failure of the current project. Sometimes the difficulties are very substantial and the young people may become so depressed or disturbed that they will fail in school or withdraw entirely from any part in the struggle. Some of them will say that they wouldn't have a date if it were to be forced on them, that it is all foolishness anyway and only the mentally deficient would be bothered with such nonsense. Let no one be fooled by that! They may show their defensiveness in other ways. Some will turn with passionate intensity to their academic work and begin to pursue a career with apparent interest and enthusiasm. Parents may be charmed by this, since it gives them a sense of relief about the boy or girl question, and the youngster's accomplishment pleases their pride. This is shortsighted, because the girl or boy can't avoid longing for the fundamental satisfactions and he won't thank his parents for overlooking his deepest longings. The wise parent will not be misled; he will try to find an answer to the youngster's difficulties and give him encouragement to stand up under momentary defeat or rejection.

If all this is so natural and expected, what of the youngster who seems to disregard the whole business and go happily about his other affairs? We must guard against any hard and fast attitude toward these things. There is, fortunately, a wide variability in the rate of development in human beings, and one must make allowances for it. For all sorts of reasons some youngsters will be in advance of their ages and some behind, but unless the advance or lag is very outstanding there is little reason to get excited. The criteria are within each child and each case has to be taken on its own merits. If a youngster is strikingly out of step in either direction, it can't be missed. The girl who insists on getting into this business at twelve and who is interested in nothing else, is certainly showing signs of strain. So is the girl who has shown no interest in it at all by the time she is seventeen. The real test is how does the youngster feel about it? If he or she is comfortable and happy and in all other ways making a good adjustment, the chances are that he is following an inner need to take things with a certain amount of caution. But if this is not the case, the youngster will show some signs of inner disturbance.

This was true of a girl who was referred for troubles which, at first glance, seemed entirely unrelated to this problem. The complaint was that she was doing badly in school. Actually this was not the difficulty at all. She was unusually large for her age, towering over most of the girls in her class. She felt awkward and ugly and undoubtedly this feeling was communicated to her associates, making them uncomfortable. She was extremely unhappy because she received no attention from the boys in her class, never had any dates, and could not endure the prospect of the coming festivities in school, which were all boy-girl affairs. She had finally made up her mind that she would devote herself to some high endeavor which would set her apart and give her the distinction that she felt she so sorely lacked. Her poor performance in school was much more apparent than real, since she showed very decided distinction in many parts of her schoolwork and devoted far too much time to it. It was fortunate for her that she was unable to pull off her plan entirely. Otherwise her misery would have been overlooked and she would not have got the help she wanted. Her mediocre school performance brought her unhappiness into the open; and with help she was able to overcome her difficulties and gradually to assume a comfortable position with her associates.

The same thing can happen in the same way to boys, and often does. With boys, however, the situation is even less apparent, because the boy is presumably making a choice and the assumption is that if he chooses not to enter into this part of the enterprise he is refraining of his own volition and is perfectly happy about it. This is often far from being so. The author saw a boy who, even at seventeen, could not be cajoled, driven, or dragged, into the vicinity of a girl. He vowed that he found them odious and boring and that he would certainly never voluntarily have anything to do with them. His parents were disposed to be tolerant and took the position that Ted would get around to it when he was ready. But when he began to show symptoms and signs of anxiety and a real reluctance to be away from his parents, they became sufficiently disturbed to seek help for him.

Deep down the truth was very very different from what it appeared to be on the surface. This boy longed for the association of girls and avoided them only out of great fear.

He had grown up in a family with two brothers younger than himself. His parents had not accepted him easily and he felt rejected when his younger brothers were born and took the major share of his parents' attention. His father especially paid him little attention and often belittled him. His mother gave him much greater acceptance and thus fostered in him an extreme attachment to her. He grew up essentially lonely and intensely unsure of himself, feeling inadequate and undesirable. When he began to meet the stresses of adolescence he ran headlong into the effects of his early life. He could not easily relinquish his attachment to his mother and therefore could not express a drive toward any woman. Furthermore, he had no identity with his father and was convinced that he would fail, be belittled and humiliated in any attempt to assert himself as a man. So, with bold defensiveness, he relinquished the whole business. But as the pressure became greater, the conflict between his wish to move toward sexual satisfaction and the doubts and fears engendered by his guilt became intolerable and neurotic anxiety appeared.

As soon as the dating age is well under way parents will observe a decided increase in the preoccupation of these youngsters with their appearance. Clothes make the girl at this time more than ever, and parents may as well prepare themselves for some attitudes that will seem unreasonable. The more doubtful and insecure the young girl feels, the more exacting she is apt to be about her dress. Dress now is a combination disguise and shield. Above all, as we have seen earlier, she feels a need to conform—to have and wear what everyone else is having and wearing. The issue of cosmetics has probably long since been settled, and the argument has boiled down to how much instead of what or whether. Girls often have a tendency to exaggerate the business of make-up until they look frighteningly like ladies of easy virtue. They have to find their way around and their argument is that if some is good, more is better. They will learn. Boys too are deeply concerned with how they look at this age; they will be as exacting and unyielding in their demands as their sisters, for they are equally dependent upon the proper appearance.

Dating, then, is only a tentative move to put the toe into the water, as it were, and does not include any wish to go for a swim. The child himself has many hesitations about tackling a problem as difficult and taxing as the sexual enterprise. In the simplest possible words, he is afraid of his own ability to handle his impulses, afraid of giving up the protection and attachment which must be relinquished if he is to establish an independent life, afraid of losing his parents' love, afraid of consequences, afraid of failure.

The next stage is "going steady." Dating has been characterized by a variety of associates and the most natural thing, of course, is out of this variety to make a selection of one and stick to that selection. Parents will immediately see that this represents a further advance and a much more serious state of affairs. It is signalized in various ways, sometimes by the boy's giving the girl a club pin. However it is demonstrated, it is a known fact in the group to which the youngster belongs. In many ways the term itself is misleading, for if there is one thing more characteristic than another about "going steady" it is that it is not at all steady. The author knew a young girl, who was in no sort of difficulty, who managed to "go steady" with ten different boys in the course of one school term. However, it is a serious matter while it lasts and, symbolically, represents an attempt to simulate the final faithful mating.

"Going steady" is likely to arouse considerable antagonism in parents, because they feel that it is much too close to the real thing and believe that the young person will have a much better chance to find a proper partner if he does not confine himself too early to one associate. They also are alarmed because they quite properly believe that X marks the spot where physical contact is likely to begin, and there is the rub. At this point a girl, especially, is faced with the question to pet or not to pet. Petting and necking are not necessarily synonymous, petting being usually the less serious. It is the girl who must face the problem, for the boy is the one who initiates it in most instances, and it is the girl's privilege to accept it or reject it as she wishes to. However upset most parents may be at their youngster's arrival at this stage of his development, they will have to make some adjustment to it; for the author is certain that this kind of activity is universal today. The real problem is not how to stop it but how to prepare the youngster to handle it.

Its beginnings are very mild indeed, usually involving a little kissing, some limited caressing and fondling. The problem of course around any sexual play is that of extent. It is obvious to any adult, but far less obvious to the youngster, that sexual play is designed to lead to greater and greater intimacy and finally to intercourse. Youngsters are often very cocksure about their ability to handle "the situation." But their confidence is due to their total lack of experience and inability to project themselves into the situation which will follow. For after kissing and mild fondling will come the need for greater and greater bodily intimacy, first without exposure and then with more and more exposure. First the citadel of the girl's breasts will be permitted, and mutual handling of the entire body may follow. The author has talked to many youngsters who have quite readily told of the total intimacy short of intercourse which they permit.

Parents are in a tight spot. They realize, as the youngster cannot, the explosive nature of the situation he is in. They cannot trust the youngster's ability to handle the forces in himself that are unleashed by these progressively more intimate contacts. Their fear may make them so panicky that they can only trot out a kind of blind and determined opposition to any kind of relationship between boys and girls if they believe there is the smallest chance of intimacy. The result inevitably will be a frantic attempt to police the situation. All that can come of this is a wide rift between the parents and the child and the establishment in the child of a "resistance movement." His sexual yearning goes underground and becomes secret and furtive, and all chance at guidance, counseling and control is lost. The mother who emphatically affirms that her daughter is not under any circumstances to indulge in any form of petting is putting herself in a position where she is either going to look ridiculous or be a hopeless failure. The pressure today for physical expression between boys and girls is so omnipresent and the atmosphere of the society in which we live so permissive that we would be like a man in the jungle thumbing his nose at the oncoming tiger if we attempted to enforce such a rule. Any society which gives drivers' licenses and automobiles to boys of seventeen and allows them to take girls of the same age out in those cars is clearly in no position to police the situation. That is exactly what is going on, and there is no sign that there is a large demand for any change.

The reader may object that this sounds like a call to despair—practically to throw up one's hands and admit defeat, meanwhile allowing the young to go their own way to destruction. This is not what is meant. But facts must be faced and ways found to deal with them if we are to have any rapport between the young and their elders, who must provide guidance, counsel and control where it is necessary. Nevertheless, the parent who relies upon his authority as his only weapon is certain to fail. Relations between himself and his young will degenerate into a battle and he will miss entirely his numerous opportunities to provide the help that is wanted. It must be remembered that the child himself has many fears and hesitations about the immense task of sexual liberation. These fears hold him back. His parent may become their ally. But on the other hand, inner pressures are forcing him toward the undertaking as an imperative part of his growing up and the society in which he lives is very often the ally of those pressures. What the adolescent wants is neither blind opposition nor equally senseless permission; he wants sympathetic understanding and help where he needs it and an open door between himself and his parents. All these can be supplied by facing the facts with him clearly—the facts as they are, *not* as the parent wishes them to be.

The parent cannot deny the existence of these sexual pressures—the desire to find love, to grow up and demonstrate one's ability and achievements as a sexually mature adult. He will have to recognize with the youngster that all this is good and part of his life as it should be, not shameful or bad. But the parent will have to be the one to point up the immense responsibilities that are also involved, the need for control and thought, the danger of unhappiness if there is nothing but a helpless giving way to impulse. Finally, the parent must make it clear that he intends to go to the youngster's help and supply the lacking control through his own firmness if he thinks it is necessary. Many a youngster wants to know that. Unless he is supplied with this kind of understanding, there will almost surely be a catastrophe in the relations between him and his parents. The catastrophe will take many forms, ranging from a total lack of communication to the most outlandish and disturbing behavior.

This is particularly well illustrated by the story of a nineteen-year-old girl who was brought for treatment because her parents felt that a psychiatrist could probably make her a more satisfactory daughter. As it was, they reported, she failed entirely to live up to their wishes. They were particularly disturbed by the fact that her educational record was bad and that it seemed impossible for her to adjust properly in any school she attended. They also recognized that she was extremely unhappy, but they had no idea why this was so.

The parents' story revealed the fact that the youngster had always been provided with the proverbial "everything that money could buy." If it were dogs she wanted, dogs it was; if horses, horses; if trips, trips; and so on up to and including a psychiatrist. It was soon apparent that the girl herself felt that she had never been really loved or appreciated and that their material lavishness only concealed their real indifference. Her parents were themselves none too happy together, her father being a driving professional man who had little regard for his wife's less intellectual needs. Their marriage had been one of loneliness for both of them and each looked to the child for gratification. The situation was not helped by the fact that the girl's older brother, a compliant and obedient, if nonetheless unhappy, boy had given his parents every cause for satisfaction. When the girl reached puberty her path and that of her parents had separated. She constantly stated that she never could and never would discuss the matters closest to her, having to do with her relations with boys, with her mother. It had been made completely clear to her that such things were strictly forbidden and that she would be severely punished for any transgression. Discussion was out. Obedience was expected.

It was no surprise to discover that her first concern when seen by the author was that she was probably pregnant. This matter was so urgent that not until later could the full story of her underground life come out. When it did, it was a sad story of a long defiance of her parents' wishes and commands. Very early she had begun to permit sexual intimacies which she didn't like and didn't really want. But her anxiety to be loved by anyone had driven her to pay any price for it. Once started, she was helpless to stop and her desperation and misery were boundless. She was somewhat comforted (but the reader no doubt will be disturbed) by the fact that all the girls in her school were conducting themselves more or less similarly.

The author does not suppose that such stories are universal, but she does believe that they are frequent and altogether too commonplace to be dismissed as rare "case histories." This girl like many others was the victim of ignorance, overindulgence, and a confused mixture of feelings— the need to grow up, the craving for love, and the desire for revenge. Her story represents a state of affairs in which the normal necking and petting had all too soon given way to a complete sexual experience. One of the miserable things about such experiences is that they are so seldom even faintly satisfactory. Much more often they are sordid and incomplete attempts which leave both partners guilty and ashamed. In the case of perhaps the majority of youngsters, of course, the phase of necking and petting is lived through and not followed by sexual relations until the girl or boy is ready for them.

But it is obvious that the whole matter of adolescent sexual behavior is shrouded in ignorance and confusion, and badly lacks definition and decision. We do not know really what is going on, because relations between the adolescent and his parents are so disturbed that the information is not forthcoming. All the information that we *do* have indicates very strongly that sexual relations during the adolescent years are very commonplace and on the increase. Generally, the spoken attitude toward this is one of complete disapproval. If that disapproval is actual, then we are faced with complete bankruptcy in our attempts to make it count for anything. If the disapproval is not real, then we should abandon it.

Parents are themselves in a considerable dilemma, and no less than their children are involved in the changing mores of our times. Today every sign points toward a greatly increased laxity in the relations between the sexes, not only premaritally but intramaritally. In the *New York Times* for December 29, 1949 the following article appeared under the heading "CHANGE FORECAST IN SEX TOLERANCE—Acceptance of Wider Freedom Suggested to Sociologists as Trend to New Standards."

Our society will be "within a very few generations as tolerant of premarital but postpubertal sexual relations as are the majority of the other peoples of the world," it was predicted yesterday by Dr. George Peter Murdock, Professor of Anthropology at Yale University.

He was one of a panel of speakers on family research before the American Sociological Society, holding its forty-fourth annual session at Manhattan Center under the auspices of the American Association for the Advancement of Science.

Emphasizing that his own role was not to "advocate" the change, Dr. Murdock said:

"I am merely making a cold, inescapable scientific prediction that our society is trending in that direction. As a scientist, I am forced to predict the disappearance of old standards and also to acknowledge that new standards, even if personally unwelcome, probably will work out to the satisfaction of everyone."

Dr. Murdock said he was "not personally apprehensive" over the rising divorce rate.

"Many societies have produced satisfactory cultural adjustment to what is technically known as 'brittle marriage,'" he added. "Moreover, I suspect that increasing premarital freedom may ultimately lead to more rational selection of mates and thereby to a decline in divorce."

Judging by comparable societies, Dr. Murdock said he could see "no grounds for expecting American women to slough off all or most of their domestic economy and child-bearing duties." But, he said, they could still assume a much larger role in economic and professional life.

"Our society is still well below the world average in the non-domestic roles that are open to women," he declared.

Dr. Mirra Komarovsky, Associate Professor of Sociology at Barnard College, suggested that the more sheltered upbringing of a girl, as compared with that of a boy, creates such ties to the parental family that she is handicapped in marriage and requires a shift of primary loyalty to a family of her own.

This difference in the early training of the sexes, she said, is widely believed to prepare girls for their future roles. But a result of it, she said, was that women frequently remain "more infantile, submissive and dependent, and less able to make their own decisions and to face their parents' disapproval" in conflict with the interests with their own husbands and children.

While psychiatrists have advanced the Elektra and Oedipus theories, she contended that more study should be given to the effect of early training in a cultural pattern.

The wishful thinking that inclines all parents to believe that the problem exists somewhere outside their own responsibilities, their indecision, their lip service to the old ideas, their stubborn refusal to face the facts, all add to the current confusion. Consider the obvious nonsense in the commonly accepted way of life for today's adolescent. He is given strictly to understand that he or she is expected to be good, that the parents will disapprove of any sexual misbehavior. All kinds of danger is presumed to exist in sexual laxity, and warnings are rife. But the same parent sees nothing absurd in giving young people all sort of opportunities for the most unrestricted intimacies and at the same time expecting them to refrain from taking advantage of those opportunities.

Young people are not strong enough for this kind of thing. It is placing upon them a burden which is heavier and more demanding than they can tolerate. We don't expect two-year-olds to tackle the jobs of eight-year-olds, but we find nothing strange in expecting thirteen-year-olds to tackle jobs that are difficult for nineteen-year-olds. Their impulses and wishes are too strong for them. To leave them without help in dealing with these impulses and all the pressures which they are subject to from the outside world is no better than desertion. Young people deserve better than that. They are hard pressed from all sides and they are looking for some direction, some help, something to hang on to and be sure of. They don't see too much assurance in the adults around them, who themselves often don't seem to know where they are going.

Are we perhaps making a fuss about nothing? Would it be just as well to interfere not at all with the sexual activities of the young and let "nature take its course"? Does a situation that encourages sexual intimacies between youngsters in adolescence promote adult stability, make for solid and enduring marriages and give emotional balance? Or does it injure their chances for later happiness, make marital adjustment more difficult, and foster a state of chaotic irresponsibility? In other words, does it hurt or help the child and does it hurt or help society? The author believes that no open-and-shut answer can be given. It depends upon a number of qualifying factors. The age of the youngster, his emotional organization at the time, his underlying motives, the meaning which such relations have for him, all must be taken into account. It is safe to assert that with the rarest possible exceptions a youngster in his middle teens cannot possibly handle the immense impact of sexual experience. Development has simply not reached the point at which the individual is prepared to undertake so difficult and confusing an enterprise. For the most part sexual activity in these early years before eighteen can only be an expression of confusion and conflict which is disturbing the orderly growth process. Some of it is an expression of hostility and defiance toward parents. Some of it is a search for secure love. Whatever its motivation, it will lead only to chaos and misery.

These arguments apply to both boys and girls but with greater force to girls. In the female, sexual involvement is more total and more ultimate than in the male. At the basis of this fact is the biological circumstance of pregnancy which has formed and impressed the female personality. Woman has a much greater tendency to invest her total self in a sexual relation, and she is inevitably more vulnerable. Therefore, she is going to feel an acute anguish when she is disappointed and abandoned. No one who has any experience with these matters can help being struck by the regularity with which the young boy will turn away from and desert his early sexual partners. Too frequent disappointment can lead by easy stages to a kind of frenzied search for security and love which may develop into a pattern of promiscuous disorder. And the girl herself, of course, may be vacillating and unstable and unable to maintain an attachment even if the boy proves capable of it.

Whether there is abandonment on either side or not, the girl is torn by a very disturbing internal conflict. The feeling that she is doing wrong and violating some deep and binding code is more often than not inescapable. Her fear of punishment and fear of losing her parents' love are equally great. So she is forced to keep the affair secret and is left without any guidance and without any support. Many times her emotional disturbance is so great that she is simply swept along, unable to bring herself and the situation under control. If this lack of control continues, there is a subtle undermining of the girl's integrity. She is starting to establish a pattern which she may later find difficulty in abandoning. For, if the solution to unhappiness and anxiety is found in easy recourse to sexual relations, it is probable that she will turn to that solution again and again.

The young boy has problems of his own which will interfere with his successful management of a sexual relationship. His difficulties are apt to center around a confusion in his attitude toward his partner. He has been brought up to believe that there are two kinds of girls—"good" and "bad."

"Bad girls" are those who have sexual relations before marriage. Though more often than not, he will have relations with a girl whom he has known all his life and who is obviously not "bad," he will not be able to free himself entirely of this feeling. Some of it will stick, and he may not be able to control his own disapproval of what she is doing. It may even be impossible for him to avoid feeling that she is less desirable because she has given in to his wishes for sexual intimacy. Then he can't help being ashamed of himself for feeling that way. Suffering from guilt over what he has done to the girl, even while he can't stop himself from doing it, he may be driven into the unhappy position of knowing that he himself helped, by seducing her, to bring about the situation which finally resulted in his deserting her. The results of being caught in this unmanageable welter of emotions may reach far into the adult lives of the youngsters involved and their ability to develop comfortable and secure marriages may be profoundly affected.

Many times, of course, such behavior is the earliest index of a deep and destructive inner conflict which will yield to nothing but psychiatric treatment. But often it is the result of almost fortuitous circumstances. This is where parents can function. They can determine their position, make that position clear and put their energies into seeing to it that their youngsters are held firmly in line. Parents who turn over to adolescents the entire conduct of their lives, exercising no jurisdiction and no control, can scarcely be surprised when the youngsters go overboard. Some adolescents are merely rather disturbed and shaky in these early years. If they have the firm guidance and help of solid parental conviction and devotion, they will not fall into relationships which they later regret. Once they have got into them, it is often hard for them to extricate themselves. Many who might fall into trouble, if prevented by parental care from carrying out their momentary impulses, might well go on to stronger and more satisfactory development.

In the matter of the older adolescent the situation may well be very different. Uncomfortable as the idea may be, the author believes that there is an irreversible trend in the direction of sexual relations prior to marriage during the last part of the teens and early twenties. Nor does it appear that there is necessarily any serious objection to this state of affairs. No doubt such a statement looks inflammatory and sounds like an invitation to license. But it seems to the author a fair statement of what is a fact and what must therefore be dealt with. A good many of these youngsters, particularly by the time they are twenty, are prepared to enter into a sexual relation. Under the circumstances it seems far wiser to be prepared to give these youngsters counsel, sympathy, understanding and guidance in their early sexual experiences than resolutely to turn a hypocritical back. Obviously, this had best be done cautiously, since it certainly contains hazards. Countless numbers of young people are seeking the advice of elders other than their parents in these critical moments. They do so almost universally with the tragic refrain, "I couldn't tell my mother." Many times these early experiences, though temporary, are nevertheless instructive and valuable, and gradually lead to firm convictions about a possible marital consideration that is extremely heartwarming. They are usually serious. Before we allow ourselves to insist that such behavior is outrageous or forbidden we should remember that in different times these youngsters would have been safely married. So it is not the sexual experience that we object to but the circumstance in which it takes place.

To parents who want to be a positive factor in their youngsters' lives and exert a constructive influence on their early sexual experience, I would suggest that these points be kept firmly in mind:

1. Training for a mature femininity or masculinity doesn't begin at puberty. It begins when the child is born. It is part of every parent's responsibility to know and understand that everything he or she does is helping or hindering the development of the child.

2. Specific sexual instruction is a life-long matter too, and begins with the first question, "Where do I come from?"

3. The adolescent's impression of his parents' attitude toward the relation between men and women will have a far greater effect on his own attitude than any amount of book learning or academic instruction.

4. By the time that puberty is reached, and increasingly during adolescence, youngsters are aware of and driven by a sexual need which is normal, desirable and healthy.

5. They cannot be expected to manage their own impulses unaided.

6. Parents will have to be prepared to take an active hand in the relationship between boys and girls in the early teens. Even at the risk of unpopularity and downright hostility, they should exercise steady jurisdiction and control over boys and girls of this age to prevent their entering into premature sexual activity.

7. The control should not be furtive, nor should it be allowed to degenerate into a cops and robbers game. Parents must share their convictions with their youngsters and discuss them openly. Adolescents are intelligent and reasonable human beings who respond to reasonable parental attitudes far better than to blustering and coercion. They are entitled to enter into their parents' thinking and have a part in the planning and adoption of the parental attitude.

8. Fundamentally, these youngsters must understand, and above all parents must believe, that sexuality is a vital part of life and one to which young people have a right to look forward. The reasons for its early control

are perfectly understandable to boys and girls themselves. They welcome the strong arm of the parents as an aid to their own sometimes flimsy self-control.

9. The later part of adolescence probably brings with it the need for parental acceptance of premarital sexual relations. Sympathetic and realistic understanding and acceptance of the situation will go far toward helping the young person to show prudence and discretion, and to avoid foolish and dangerous activity.

If these counsels of perfection, or even a good part of them, can be heeded, we will see fewer of the tragic messes that so many of today's young people make of their lives. There will be a strengthening of relationships between them and their parents and a deepening of mutual sympathy and understanding. The youngsters' lives will be safer and more comfortable, and the parents will be freed of a great deal of their anxiety and apprehension. These young people are properly engaged in sexual growing up. No reasonable parent can deny that fact or wish it not to be true. To turn one's back, to oppose it blindly, to invoke every sanction against any expression of it, can only lead to a deep alienation between the adolescent and his parents. The living process is on his side and finally that process will be served.

IX

Delinquency

Unhappily, no story of the adolescent can be complete without a discussion of the delinquencies of this age. So extensive and so disturbing has the problem become in the last twenty years that it is not uncommon immediately to associate delinquency with the word adolescence. No other possible teen-age development causes parents greater concern, for inevitably it brings with it shame and disgrace and an overwhelming sense of failure.

There are no forms of adult delinquency that are not from time to time practiced by the young person. Even crimes of violence, though not usual, have become more frequent in recent years. We hear now, all too often, of murders committed by very young people, sometimes in their earliest teens. Sexual misbehavior, armed robbery, grand larceny, automobile theft, and other serious acts are not uncommon. The reader can compile his own list—from the newspapers, if necessary, for it is a rare day when they don't carry a story of some teen-age crime. A few years ago, a celebrated case was that of a young girl of about sixteen who had murdered her mother, ostensibly because supper was late. That obviously wasn't the reason but that was the story newspaper readers were given. Baby-sitters of tender age have killed their charges. Small boys have been reported holding up candy stores even if only with toy guns. Teen-age car robbers are not unknown by any means. More often, of course, it is the lesser crimes—petty larceny, truancy, incorrigibility, minor offenses of all kinds—that bring adolescents into contact with the authorities; but they are so frequent that they appear in the newspapers in the form of statistical tables rather than case histories. It takes murder by youthful babysitters, or suicide pacts between teen-age lovers made desperate by the girl's pregnancy, or continuous marauding by young gangs to make a news story at this point. Every large city is plagued with a variety of such crimes. Teen-age gangs, particularly, have been for some years a recognized source of delinquent behavior, and special police cadres are set up to deal with them, as with all forms of juvenile delinquency.

The lesser categories of misbehavior are perhaps neglected in the midst of more pressing problems, but they too take up an enormous amount of time and energy on the part of the social agencies involved. Truancy, for example, can rightfully be called a major difficulty because of its extent. Beginning often well before adolescence and continuing through school life, it represents the outstanding problem of the schools, and requires a special group of workers to cope with it.

Sexual delinquency is in a class by itself. Long given a high priority in the list of juvenile disasters, it is in its extent an expression of the disturbed conditions of today's living, and unquestionably one of major sores on the body of society. It is well enough defined in theory, but in practice the lines are less clear. Society as a whole seems not to know what is and what is not really delinquent. Naturally, it is only an offense if it is discovered; still more confusing, it is a much worse offense if it is discovered in a girl. But, whatever it is or isn't, and however much of it there is about, there is no doubt that it has to be dealt with in some fashion.

Admittedly this business of crime and delinquency has been with us always. So what are we to make of the present hue and cry about it? Kids have been playing hooky since there have been kids, and schools to play hooky from; youngsters have been stealing as long as there has been property; girls have been having illegitimate babies and everyone has been horrified about it for uncounted generations; and there have been "bad" youngsters in every community from time immemorial. So we must ask ourselves what the present-day to-do about it indicates.

The first significant point is that there is an absolute increase in antisocial behavior. A larger proportion of young people and children are showing signs of delinquency today than in the past. The second important point is that today's tightly knit city community makes delinquency much more dangerous and more difficult to deal with than it ever was before. When the occurrence was relatively rare and took place in small homogeneous communities or rural areas, it was easier to handle. The parents or the social group as a whole did what was needed. When the older ways of coping with such problems proved no longer feasible, some organized approach became necessary, and has in fact developed. For juvenile delinquency has assumed proportions too intolerable, and has become too dangerous to too many people, to be dealt with any longer in informal and unorganized ways.

In order to high-light these facts, let us look at some fairly haphazard statistics, taking due account of the fact that they have certain defects. These figures come from the *Uniform Crime Reports* compiled by the F.B.I., Department of Justice, from fingerprint arrest records forwarded by states and municipalities (including only state and municipal offenses). They must of necessity be regarded as extremely conservative because many such fingerprint cards are not forwarded to Washington, and for a second more weighty reason—the fairly widespread reluctance to make arrest records of juvenile persons.

	Percentage of Persons Under 25 and Over 10 Years of Age in the Total Population	Percentage of Arrests of Persons under 25 to Total Arrests Made
1949	22.5	31.2
1948		31.8
1947		33.4
1946	23.9	34.2
1945	23.2	35.6
1944	24.1	36.1
1943	25.2	36.0
1942	26.0	32.4
1941	26.6	
1940	26.0*	32.7
1935	27.2	37.0
1930	26.0*	

* Estimated—figures incomplete

Predominant Age of All Arrests of All Persons and All Types of Offense

1949	21 years
1946	21
1945	17
1944	17
1943	18
1942	18
1941	19
1940	19
1939	19
1938	21
1937	22

The figures that follow are also revealing in respect to the juvenile:

In 1949: persons under 25 represented 54.1% of those charged with robbery, 59.5% of those charged with burglary, 44.8% of those charged with larceny, 67.0% of those charged with auto theft, about 50.0% of those charged with all crimes against property.

Whatever these figures mean, and admitting that they are not "accurate" in the exact sense of the word, they are not reassuring. As an indication, if we wish to take them only as that, they point to grave difficulties of social adjustment in the young person not yet mature or only in the very earliest stages of maturity.

So delinquency has become a public responsibility, which means that to a very large extent it has become the delegated concern of groups of experts who are presumed to be specially trained to deal with the problem effectively. These include: the courts and all the agents of law enforcement; the schools with all their adjunct services, such as attendance control and child guidance and counseling services; the churches with their religious training; the professions which specialize in the understanding and treatment of personality difficulties: psychiatrists, psychologists, social workers and their allies. Then there are the various agencies that have come into being to deal with personal and family problems and with the particular problems of juvenile delinquency—all social agencies, for instance. In many large cities there are special courts with special services designed to work correctively with the young offender. There are also numerous clinics for treatment and correction, but they are not numerous enough. Big cities are honeycombed with community houses, neighborhood recreational projects and similar undertakings which provide counterattractions to the street activities which so easily lead to delinquency. There are police athletic leagues and big brother movements, which also help. Nevertheless, it appears that these are only after-the-fact institutions, and that somewhere along the line the right approach has been missed or our knowledge is incomplete or we simply perversely do not take the steps that we ought to.

To take the right steps, it would be necessary to be fairly sure what the causes of delinquency are. Various theories have enjoyed passing popularity over the years. The idea of natural or indwelling criminality, given expression through the work of Lombroso, was widely approved for some time and there are still strong traces of that largely unfounded belief in the minds of many people today. The notion summed up in "bad blood," which was a way of expressing the idea that the delinquent tendency was hereditary, has had a good deal of popularity. In folkloristic attitudes today there is still found considerable allegiance to this idea.

Poverty and slum conditions, which were the natural consequences of urban life, have long been thought to be breeders of crime. At this point there was for some time a dead stop. Since the obvious answer to that theory was somehow to better the conditions under which the so-called slum child grew up, the following years saw the emergence of all kinds of activities designed to offset the deprivations to which these youngsters were subjected. This theory, however, has not survived in its original form. There is no reason to be less concerned about the way in which huge numbers of city people are obliged to live, but it is necesary to revise our attitude toward the consequences. Too many slum dwellers fail to become delinquent to make that the entire answer. Also, it was soon obvious that a large number of children who did not suffer from the ill effects of slum life also became delinquent. Some of these did not, and today still do not, come to the attention of the authorities because their families possess the means and the knowledge to handle the situation without allowing the civil authorities to enter in. Truancy is a different matter in a child attending a private school than it is in the case of a child in the public schools. So is petty stealing or, for that matter, more serious stealing when the parents can make restitution. Sexual delinquency does not come to the attention of the agencies equipped to deal with it when the parents can arrange to take care of its consequences in illegitimate pregnancies.

Theory after theory has been examined and abandoned as the absolute and final cause of all delinquency. More and more, emphasis has been directed toward the deeper question of the personality of the youngster who is involved or may become involved in trouble. The older theories have not been entirely abandoned, but their place in the causal chain has been modified. There may be, and probably are, certain individuals who inherently are easily influenced toward antisocial attitudes and acts. But that is only part of the story. There surely are reasons in the deprivations and cruelties of city slums for the individual to turn on the society which allows them to exist. That is still only part of the story. The basic problem is one of personality, and that, in turn, depends on the kind of rearing the child has had. This is not a question, entirely or even largely, of material wealth, but of emotional qualities and especially of family relationships.

These ideas were given their first really organized expression by August Aichhorn, to whom all workers in this field must look as the "prophet" of their cause. Aichhorn was a teacher working in Vienna who became enormously impressed by the theories of Sigmund Freud. He began to apply those theories to young people with whom he came in contact who were delinquent or were about to become so. Aichhorn was able to demonstrate through many brilliant studies that the difficulties which these youngsters displayed very often arose from the unsolved inner conflicts which had been brought into existence by the early circumstances of their development. Unsocial behavior could then be seen at last as an outlet for repressed emotion or as a solution of otherwise insoluble conflicts, the expression of a neurotic attitude. Much of what we know now about the ways of coping with behavior problems comes directly from these early insights of Aichhorn's.

In addition to the factors of personality, which are particular for each individual, the author feels that there is today a cultural force assailing every individual, to which certain susceptible ones succumb. This can be described as a disturbance and disorder of society in which old strengths are immensely vitiated and therefore no longer available to feed and sustain the family and the youngsters who must grow up in it. The culture is the medium in which the social and emotional life of the individual has its being. It conditions all attitudes, personal and institutional, and its effect is everywhere.

Today many of the components of our culture are intensely exaggerated, anxiety being the emotion that most notably characterizes our society. Everyone is anxious; the whole of society is anxious, as its behavior and reactions testify. The anxiety arises from many sources, but it is essentially a fear centering around the threat to survival—physical, social, economic, emotional. Of all the factors contributing to this feeling, the most outstanding is the keynote of industrial society—competitiveness. This competitiveness has its origin in the economic structure but finds its expression in all parts of life.

The greater this factor in any situation, the greater the possibility of failure. In economic failure, there is a direct blow at security. Competitiveness here is not only very intense but it is all-pervasive. Unless the individual is willing and able to cope with the situation as it is, there is no way in which he can earn his living. And without that fundamental guarantee, there is no security. A man today cannot enter adult life secure in the feeling that he will have a job if he is willing to work and that he has every prospect of keeping that job and building a safe and comfortable life for his family. Too many unpredictables enter into it. Neither he nor anyone else can tell when the business cycle may reverse itself. There may be so much competition that he will be crowded out. The special training which is more and more necessary today may not be available to him. Or others may be better trained.

Even if he gets a good job, he is liable to be beset with the fear that it isn't good enough. For today it is necessary to achieve a special position if one is to feel secure. All sorts of work are better than all sorts of other work. It is "better" to be in the white collar class than an artisan. Why this is "better" is pretty hard to discover but it is so nevertheless. If a man earns a good living, he must earn a better. This is called advancement. Where it is advancement *to* is a question for anyone who would like to answer it, but advancement is a fetish in today's world. Presumably it means to get to a position where security is unassailable. Since this is not actually possible and everyone feels, of necessity, the underlying uncertainty of modern life, there is no end to the pressure for more and more of the same. Today's standards of living are so high that everyone is put to it to keep up. For "high" read "costly" and the sentence is closer to the truth.

Then, beside the actual job and the holding of it, everyone has to contend with the problem of prestige. This elusive commodity is very hard to define as it is used in today's world, but it is definite and deeply felt. More or less, it has come to mean the possession of influence or power or charm.

Whatever it is, it is enormously valuable and everyone strives for it. It is something that belongs to bank presidents and moving picture stars, to ball players and bishops, to people who live in the "right places" and people who do the wrong things in the right way, to the "best-dressed men" and the "best-dressed women" and a thousand others. It is importance; it is being recognized on the street and asked for your autograph; it is being recognized by the right headwaiters; it is having the right kind of job; it is being on first-name relations with the great and near great. It is getting places and being somebody. To be an artisan or a craftsman is far less estimable than to be a white collar worker, even though the former may earn more money. The gradations are quite exact and clearly understood, though never openly admitted. To achieve professional status is one of the aspirations of those born in the lower middle classes. To earn a great deal of money is an aspiration that only the professional classes have been able to forego.

What one does to attain all these things has a precise and definite effect upon one's self-esteem as well as upon one's security. It is often difficult to determine which drive is more potent, for it is easy to observe that many times there will be an actual sacrifice of security in order to achieve the position and status which the striving for prestige demands.

This is nicely demonstrated by the way in which young people, whether or not they have any special interests or aptitudes, will rush to get a college education. It provides a kind of superior rating which may be translated into job security as well as into position. It may do no such thing, for if the individual's aptitude is so slight as to make the effort and cost disproportionately great, he may simply sacrifice everything else to the prestige value of a college education. The general attitude of those who have omitted to take this precaution is one of apologetic deference to their supposedly superior brethren who have done so.

For some happy individuals, all this striving and struggling seem to be easy, and they are notably successful at whatever they set their hands to. What internal price they pay is not easily apparent, but the fact that many of them succumb to those very diseases that are the product of strain is certainly not coincidental. More numerous are the people who do find the struggle very difficult. Their need to succeed and achieve is overweening, but their ability to do so and their inner strength are not equal to the task. This discrepancy can lead to all sorts of activities that are fundamentally designed to secure the rewards without the really necessary effort. Many of these methods are dubious or even disreputable. Corner-cutting and minor forms of dishonesty have therefore become the idiom of the time rather than unusual and punishable offenses. Where money and position are the criteria of success, no sacrifice and no activity will be too great. These circumstances—the rapidly increasing closeness of competition and the steadily greater threat which that means—have served to bring about a situation in society that is perilously close to anarchy. Anything goes, no matter what form of moral shoddiness is involved. The thing is to get on, and the way in which it is done is far less important than to do it. In such a moral climate, the delineations between the acceptable and unacceptable, the right and the wrong, are very shady.

It is into this moral climate that the adolescent emerges. It is impossible for him to escape knowledge of the kind of thing that is going on all around him. It is communicated to him by every part of his world. All too often he is well aware of the fact that, while his parents are imposing the most serious sanctions on him for his infringements of the proper code of behavior, they are themselves breaking the rules without the smallest qualm. One youngster brought this out very clearly when he said he saw no reason why he should be impressed by his parents' authority, when they shared with him the fact that they were actually engaged in black market operations. For any youngster such a situation is too much to have to deal with, and one can scarcely be surprised that their own attitudes are corrupted by the easy morality of their environment. Today, for instance, cheating has become an accepted procedure in college examinations. It is merely a matter of how well one can get on and how adroit one is in fooling the authorities. The question whether cheating is per se a proper undertaking does not enter into it. Can you get away with it or can you not? That pretty well sums up the prevailing attitude of our society. The clever people are those who will get on in the world, and they will often regard as completely idiotic the idea that to get on in this fashion is to pay too high a price.

This point of view may be bad enough but it is not what is generally meant by delinquency. Things have to get a great deal worse before anyone will broadcast an alarm. That is precisely where the difficulty lies. When there is so little interest in the beginnings of misconduct, it is easy for the young to slip further and further into dubious behavior. Today's young person who gets into the hands of the authorities, or is barely kept out of them by the efforts of his parents, will have to exert himself in the direction of substantial misbehavior. No one is delinquent who merely cheats on his income tax or examination (unless caught), but anyone who steals an automobile or who holds up a bar or shoots his little brother is unquestionably so. So also is any girl who has an illegitimate child or has a career of sexual promiscuity even though she avoids pregnancy. So, too, are the chronic truants and the pilferers as well as the unmanageable and incorrigible youngsters who rebel against the intolerable homes in which every fundamental of human decency is violated. These are the problems that are recognized and cause consternation.

Regardless of the environment in which the youngster has been reared, there can be found within him a reason for his acts, a reason that lies in his personality, which has been formed out of the injuries and conflicts with which he has had to deal in the struggle to grow up. His unsocial behavior is a reflection of those inner conflicts and his effort to solve them. It is, in short, a sickness of the personality, of the spirit. The conflict may be between the youngster's need for position and recognition and his sense of inability and insufficiency. It may represent the struggle between a deeply buried wish and his own opposition to that wish because it is forbidden. It may take place between his hostility and his attempts to control his hostility. It may be a hatred of neglectful and rejecting parents taken out upon the society of which they are representatives. It may be a twisted attempt to struggle free of an attachment to parents who refuse to accept his growing up. It may be the expression of a completely sick mind which has lost all hold on reality—a psychosis. It may be a wild desire to gain attention through acts of bravado. It may be a thousand things, but what it can almost never be is deliberate, malicious criminality without cause. Looking at these conflicts, it is easy to see that they can, and almost surely do, have their origin in the emotional atmosphere of the family in which the child developed. So we will have to look to childhood as the source of later delinquency.

Examine the first conflict, that between the need for approval and the feeling that one cannot get it. The need for approval and acceptance may be taken to be an inevitable and a valuable part of every human being's equipment. How about the feeling that one cannot get it or doesn't deserve it? This surely can be traced to the early years of the child's life when he is trying to establish his personality and develop his character. Here, family instability and parental rejection have the greatest force. The child, it must be remembered, is born wholly without any evaluation of himself. Only through the acceptance that he receives from his parents, their tender and affectionate devotion, their firm but considerate discipline can he acquire a sense of worth. Where parental care is slipshod, grudging or nonexistent, the child cannot hope to develop the feeling of being a valuable person, for in the childhood economy one is cared for and loved in proportion as one deserves it. This is a gross fallacy, but it is a universal belief of childhood and must be taken into consideration in any attempt to understand the child.

Such circumstances as a broken home and desertion by a parent are of enormous consequence. Nor does a parent literally have to desert the child in order to make the child feel deserted. The parent who is indifferent, for example, preoccupied with his own wishes, and cavalier toward the child's demands produces the same feeling of abandonment and lack of value—a feeling which will last the child his life long. Divorce is a potent force. There can never be a breakup in the home without the child's feeling that he has been deserted by one or another parent. Actually, that is what happens. He loses the invaluable and irreplaceable contact with the departed parent. The weekly visit, the daily telephone call, the strenuous effort to convince him that he has not been deserted never quite suffice. For to him the parent is gone and, if he is gone, he is lost to the child.

Unable to change conditions, helpless to control them, powerless to understand them, he can only draw his own conclusions and make the best defense against them that he is able. His conclusions are often false and his defenses often the kind that lead to later difficulties. Feeling unloved and unwanted, he may, as soon as his powers permit, begin to seek compensations. This attempt may prove to be delinquent. Show-off and exhibitionistic tendencies often appear. Stealing in order to provide himself with a pleasure to take the place of the lost love or to enhance his own importance and value to his associates is an easy step for such a child. And from minor thefts to the much more important ones that he is able to accomplish in adolescence is only a logical progression. Such a child is starved and angry; nor does he know the source of his own discontent. It must be shown to him through difficult investigation.

No better off is the child who is faced with the problem of a forbidden and unresolved longing left over from his infancy. This is a circumstance that lies behind a great deal of the forbidden sexual activity of adolescent girls and is the cause of many illegitimate pregnancies. Perhaps if we follow the history of one of these girls, the inevitability of the outcome will be clear. When this girl came into the office, her pregnancy was well advanced. She seemed stupefied and stunned and unable to act on her own behalf. Outwardly her pregnancy was wholly unacceptable to her, but this attitude did not seem to be in correspondence with the inner facts.

Her life's story showed a tragic deprivation. Her mother was an immature and poorly developed woman whose wish for children rested upon a shallow and insubstantial basis. No sooner were they born than she wished to be rid of them and all the trouble they caused. This girl had been separated from her father at a very early age and had never known his actual presence or his love. Her mother had neglected her always, and as soon as she began to be demanding, had sent her away to live with a relative where the girl felt herself no part of the already established family. Confused and abandoned, she could barely carry out the ordinary requirements of life. Her educational achievements were poor and her capacity to support herself inconsequential. She grew up hating the world and longing for the love of her distant father, who always seemed to her much more desirable than her lost mother.

When she encountered a man much like her father who offered her what appeared to be love, she was powerless to resist the impulses within her, and with total disregard of the consequences formed an alliance with him which ultimately resulted in her pregnancy. Her conscious attitude was one of total disgust with herself and her acts. Her entire pregnancy showed no change in this point of view and she approached her delivery with a kind of sullen hostility toward the whole thing and a determination to be rid of the child at the earliest moment possible. All this changed abruptly when the child was born. Then her longings came out in full force and she became just as determined to keep the baby as she had formerly determined to be rid of it. To act on her determination would have been to the disadvantage of both the girl and the child, since she was unable to deal with even the simplest demands of ordinary life, much less sustain herself and the child without help.

This girl had an obvious conflict centering around her father—the standard oedipal situation. The discovery of a man similar to her father and the establishment of a sexual relation with him was the obvious and inevitable solution. The guilt which such an act aroused dictated her initial determination to relinquish the baby. Then for a time that feeling gave way to her greater longing to cling to it. Finally, however, the essential immaturity of the whole project made it necessary for her to give up the child.

The girl's case was typical and illustrates a circumstance found often in both boys and girls. One of the most effective ways of seeming to deny an intolerably strong tie to the parent of the opposite sex is to enter into sexual relations with someone else at an early age. Here you have the motivation of a great deal of premature sexual activity in adolescent youngsters.

Truancy may result from a variety of causes. Sometimes the youngster feels hopelessly outclassed by his superior schoolmates and can't bear the sense of inadequacy which his failures produce. Sometimes he is unconsciously working out a grudge against his parents, who are, of course, wounded by his truancy and helpless to do anything about it. Sometimes, of course, the school is so badly suited to the child's needs and abilities that there is, in logic, no reason why he should attend, and he simply takes matters into his own hands. This may happen when parents, having developed their own notion of what the youngster should do, try to force him into a pattern for which he is not fitted. But more often truancy is a protest against conditions much closer to home.

This was the case with a youngster in the early part of adolescence who took to truancy and, still worse, to running away. His parents, grossly maladjusted, could provide him with no sort of security. His father was a broken reed indeed, being almost completely unable to cope with the demands of reality. He had had adequate training in college but had been unable to adjust himself to the necessities of marriage and family life. He was a constant "truant" himself, frequently staying away from home, and offering the boy no love. The boy's mother turned desperately to her son for help and comfort, and his attachment to her was boundless. But it was also guilty. His father's career looked like a failure to him. He, however, was too weak and helpless to take over the tasks of the man of the house. It was too long to wait until he grew up and could rescue his mother, so, since nothing offered any solution to his most pressing problems, he had no choice but to run away. In doing this, he not only escaped the miseries of home, with all its disappointments, but he also set in motion a search for the lost father. This search was enormously dangerous for it was heavily overcast with homosexual longings. When he was offered a chance to go away to school where his talents were appreciated and his problems were removed, he was able to adjust happily and comfortably and to master his difficulties. It is pleasant to note that his parents, when they saw his unhappiness, were able to mobilize themselves on his behalf.

Certain rather spectacular delinquencies in adolescence may be connected with a kind of violent, hostile need for self-assertion—on the part of the boy, for example, the bravado about his masculinity that carries him into any sort of activity necessary to prove it. It is here, of course, that gang formations are of particular importance, since they offer the best arena for the display of self-assertiveness. The gang itself represents a standard group and often demands of the youngster accomplishments which he cannot produce, or challenges him to the delinquent acts that are the standard of the group. A poorly organized youngster in these circumstances may be drawn into misbehavior out of his own weakness and insufficiency and his inability to withstand the taunts and jibes of his companions.

Undoubtedly many of the young car robbers and hold-up artists come to their criminal acts from just this kind of setting. The important thing to understand about them is that they are, all of them, suffering from a greater or lesser conflict which they can solve only in these terms. Many of them have grown up in homes where they have been so outrageously rejected and humiliated that they are fired by a determination to revenge themselves upon the society of which their parents were representatives. In stealing, particularly, they are sometimes making restitution to themselves for the love they have never had and have identified with material possessions. Early childhood stealing is very often of this sort, minor pilfering, usually from parents and usually of objects of value or of money.

There is a type of delinquent that is designated as an "incorrigible minor." This means that the boy or girl is absolutely defiant of any control that the parent may attempt to exercise. These youngsters often refuse to pay the least attention to family regulations. They will, for instance, stay away from home all night or for days at a time, refusing to tell what they were doing or where they have been. They will deliberately, and with defiant sullenness, set about to violate every regulation. Youngsters of this sort are suffering from extreme deprivation. This kind of antisocial behavior is particularly disturbing, of course, because it is a preliminary to sexual misconduct. Cases of this sort are so numerous in any and every walk of life that they have a kind of over-all similarity.

A girl whose mother had given her nothing but abuse and humiliation, who was told that she was not wanted in the home which the mother was maintaining with a man not the girl's father, took to wandering about at night, sleeping in doorways, picking up with gangs of similar youngsters, and was finally brought to court as an incorrigible minor. Actually, the incorrigibility was within the mother rather than within the girl. The difficulty in such cases is that the youngsters have been so thoroughly disillusioned in all the adults with whom they have come in contact that it is often nearly impossible to gain their confidence. In order to help them, as Aichhorn has pointed out, it is imperative that the youngster have confidence in the person trying to help him. No effort can succeed otherwise; and if the child has been too badly damaged by his past experiences, he will be unable to place his reliance in any adult and probably go on to a full-fledged criminal career. Working with these children and helping them to struggle their way back to socially accepted ways of expressing themselves is a long, laborious task which requires infinite patience and persistence.

This kind of behavior, like all sick and undesirable sorts, has its beginning in the inner conflicts of the individual. To describe all the possible variations of conflicts which can lead to sexual disorder would consume the space of many books much longer than this one. Only a sketch of the most obvious types can be suggested here. All of them have a common basis—anxiety. The boy or girl may be beset by a great deal of fear about his or her attachment to the parent of the opposite sex, for example. To give the lie to it, they may undertake sexual activity at an unsuitably early age, under improper circumstances or in clearly unhappy ways. It is as if the boy or girl were saying to the forces within himself, "I cannot really love mother (father) too much

since I am having relations with girls (boys) who clearly
are not mother (father)." It is hardly necessary to point out
the desperate nature of such an undertaking and how poorly
it proves what it sets about to prove. Love of a parent that
is so powerful that such extreme measures are required to
combat it is almost certainly going to be a powerful disturbing force in later life.

Again, there may be a corroding doubt in the unconscious
mind of the youngster about his or her masculinity or femininity. Anything like that can all too easily lead to the
obvious pragmatic solution: "Go and prove it." To the mistaken mind of such youngsters, the mere accomplishment
of sexual contact will prove it, for the moment, until the
anxiety arises anew to require a repetition of the same treatment. A parent who clearly doesn't believe in or approve of
the sexuality of the child sets in motion a train of interior
events which can logically lead to some such conclusion.
From the beginning, children must know that their intrinsic
sexuality is pleasing to their parents and that those parents
wish them to possess it and all its satisfactions—or they will
surely be plagued all their lives long.

Both boys and girls may have the feeling that sexuality
is basically indecent. Since this is a common attitude and one
of long standing, he may well wonder how, if this is so, it
can lead to such disastrous consequences. It is a matter of
the degree of intensity. The notion that sex is a necessity
for the best development of the individual comes into sharp
conflict with the idea that it is a dirty business. In spite of
all kinds of instruction to the contrary, and all the findings
of those who, like Freud, have sought out the facts of the
human personality, this idea dies hard. It is still widely current. Under the circumstances, it isn't hard to see the logic
of the argument that if it is a dirty affair, one had best
carry it out in a dirty way, with others who are as sordid as
oneself.

Some boys and girls are drawn into early or disorderly sexual activity out of a need for love, so great that it is the overmastering drive of their personalities. To the youngster who has never been loved (or thinks he has not, which is the same thing), nothing can be so precious and nothing can be too costly to give in exchange. Moreover, such people are easily deceived. Their very desire to find this priceless treasure may make them believe they have found it almost anywhere. The most palpable deceit will never be apparent to them if it is dressed in the garments of love. These wretched, hungry young people are wanderers, perpetually seeking the answer to their needs, giving themselves over to the most dangerous activities, never at home, never satisfied, always bewildered and defeated.

What everybody would like to know is how to prevent this development and how to deal with it if it occurs. Prevention is much easier and more profitable than cure, of course, and the same care that will prevent any other emotional difficulty will prevent delinquency. The best prevention is the provision to every child of a loving and secure home in which his relations with his parents are untarnished by anxiety or hostility. This is a large order today, especially when so many marriages appear to be made anywhere but in heaven and to represent less a serious contract than a plan for the promotion of pleasure to the two parties to it. Many people seem to feel that they have carried out their obligation to their children by preparing them elaborately for the breakup, rather than by trying to make their marriage steady and durable. Books are read, psychiatrists are consulted, plans laid, and all done according to the best precepts. If, in fact, the parents were as concerned about their children as these preparations would indicate, they might well expend some of the same energy in an effort to keep the marriage going. This doesn't mean that marriages that are finally insupportable are not better broken than limpingly maintained. It does mean that many marriages could be saved if the good will and energy of the parents were directed to that end.

In the homes that are intact there must be a realistic and careful attention to the needs of the youngsters in it. It isn't enough simply to maintain a home as a kind of symbol of respectability and solidity. It has to function as one. Parents must work at it and not abdicate their responsibilities to any of the multifarious agencies which have sprung up to fill the breach. It is through the years when the child is preparing to leave the home that he most needs to feel it solid and powerful around him. This means love and demand; privilege and responsibility; growing freedom and necessary discipline.

There has been a tendency, which is almost wholly destructive, to believe that acceptance of a child implies giving him complete control of his own actions, without any regulation. Children are only confused by such nonsense. They feel deserted. In part, this belief has arisen from a mistaken notion of what is meant by giving the child freedom. Freedom doesn't mean anarchy. Sometimes parents adopt this attitude because it is easier, and then assure themselves that they are doing the right thing—because "everybody says you shouldn't restrict a child." Or they may adopt it out of an honest conviction that this is the way to heaven. However, they soon learn that this particular path leads in the opposite direction. Children are too weak, too inexperienced, too dependent, to make final judgments about themselves and their conduct. They accept regulation as a natural part of parental love and care if it isn't arbitrary or capricious or simply a means of depriving them of the experience necessary to growth. The very small boy in the cartoon summed up this dilemma very aptly when he turned to his little friend and said, "Do we have to do what we want to do again today?"

Children want and expect to be helped to know what is good and what bad, what permissible and what not. Their own controls are not strong enough to keep them from giving way to impulses that actually distress them. "No" is a good and important word and, introduced at the right moment, may save a lot of trouble. A wishy-washy "Why don't you decide?" may be all that is needed to encourage the youngster to go ahead with some piece of foolishness which everybody will regret. Sometimes there can be no replacement for the absolute command or the absolute denial. It may come at the most irksome time, but that may be precisely when it is needed. If the parents see plainly that a certain course of action is going to be more than the young boy or girl can handle, and is likely to lead him into experiences that will be too much for him, they are as obligated to put a stop to it as one is obligated to flag down a train when one knows there is a washed-out bridge ahead. The interdiction may be received with sullen anger and outcries about freedom, but these will have to be borne as part of the game of being parents. To side-step a responsibility because it is easier to is criminal negligence.

Parents also have to take account of themselves as examples to the young. This was once a popular notion, but it has fallen off in recent years. However, it is still valid. Children and young people have to have ideals on which to model themselves. If they are to know that there is a real and solid ethical basis for life, they have to find it in their parents. This means that there cannot be any slipshod or halfhearted approach to the early signs of irresponsible behavior; that every sign (and there will be many) of failure to live up to certain simple rules of right and wrong must be looked at and dealt with straightforwardly. This does not mean that one should use harshness or make exacting demands for the kind of conformity the child is unable to give. Neither does it mean that the fantasy and play of every young child should be considered lying. The fantasy life of young childhood is one of the richest sources of later creativity and to interfere with it by a stern insistence that "Fairies aren't real," "Santa Claus isn't so," and sundry other strict interpretations of the gospel of honesty is sheer stupidity. But when the parent is able to see that the child knows that what he says is an untruth, and that the untruth has to do with here-and-now reality, he must deal with it gently but firmly, insisting upon a strict regard for what is rather than what might be.

The same attitude must be taken toward all sorts of easy evasions. Neither harshness nor punitiveness will serve. What is needed is a straightforward, unswerving determination to set the matter straight more as a question of the record than for punishment. In the same way, the conscientious and understanding parent, without rigidity, will insist that the boy or girl face up to every issue. If there has been stealing, then some way must be found for the child to make up for it. If lying, then it must be corrected. If it is a question of consideration for others, their rights and needs, there can't be any compromise. A child has to learn to live in a group, co-operating and respecting the rights of others. For this, nothing can take the place of living with parents who demand of themselves more than they demand of the children and who live up to every requirement made of them. There isn't any doubt that the present-day moral evasiveness and materialistic conception of life are having a profound effect upon the young who are entering into the years of their maturing. The probity and straightforwardness, the uncompromising self-discipline, the ability to relinquish, that the parents can demonstrate to their children, will be a far more effective counterinfluence than all the preachments and arguments they can mobilize.

This is the living experience, and only out of this experience can the child organize a character that will sustain him in the demands of modern living. Clearly, the part required of the parents is considerable. First of all, they themselves have to know what it is they expect of life and what they expect to bring to it. Many times this may demand a sharp definition of things and a disagreement with the current concepts of easy living. This will not be difficult if the previous relationship with the children has been loving and strong. Children will follow where a strong and devoted leader sets the pace. No parent should be surprised if, having abdicated leadership himself, he finds his child following in paths of which he cannot approve. Nor if, having always cut corners himself he finds the same tendency in his child in an exaggerated form.

If the ideal measures fail, as sometimes they may, and evidence of delinquency appears in early adolescence, there can be but one answer, and that is immediate recourse to the facilities for expert help which the community provides. It cannot be too strongly emphasized that once there has been an overt expression of delinquent attitudes and trends, the time for half-measures is over and all preventive measures are too late. To wait, to hope, to evade, to compromise at this point is to invite disaster of the most horrifying order. Every case history of an adolescent delinquent shows with startling clarity the fact that the parents saw the situation and tried home remedies, or, worse than that, tried to cover it up. The net result was, and will always be, continuing progress toward disaster. Delinquency must be faced as an illness and dealt with as promptly as any other illness. Any attempt to fool oneself and to hope for the best is almost certain to bring a harvest of misery for both parents and children. This means that parents must be willing to go with the full story of their difficulties to those in the community who are in a position to know and understand the situation. Shame or defensiveness will result only in a postponement of the inevitable accounting. But these children can be helped

—if help is provided early enough. Inevitably parents feel that such a search on their part is an admission of failure, and they hesitate to make that admission. But they do so at their peril and the peril of the youngster involved. Only early and vigorous efforts to tackle these problems at their roots will yield the kind of results that are wanted.

Society, as it expresses itself in its institutions and agencies, its organization and attitudes, will have to take a hand in this business too. Every parent will have to believe that any delinquency in any youngster is delinquency in his own boy or girl before we can hope that this vexing business will be tackled. It is easy to read horror stories about a terrible catastrophe in a small town far away or in a neighborhood one imagines to be far different from one's own and then forget them with the complacence of the ignorant. The only treatment that occurs to such people is to be sure that they themselves live in the right part of town and prevent their youngsters from associating with the unfortunate "bad elements." Unhappily, this form of treatment is unlikely to produce any spectacular results. The problem of misbehavior isn't confined to one side of the tracks, one high school, one economic or social group, or one anything else. It is a community problem, and unless it is seen as such it will mushroom and appear in the most inappropriate places. The same people who wouldn't for a moment allow the sewage system of their town to be restricted to the people on the right side of the tracks, lest the whole community be contaminated, will composedly turn their backs on a problem of an equal magnitude when it involves the moral issue of crime.

Every power of the city or town must be mobilized to prevent delinquency, to make it unnecessary, impossible. This means that everyone concerned with the schools and churches, courts and social agencies, community houses, playgrounds and other recreational facilities, guidance centers, medical facilities, housing, adult education, and newspapers, as well as the citizens themselves, will have to make it their own affair to see to it that what is needed is provided. All the influences to which the young person is subjected, beginning with the family and spreading in widening circles to embrace all elements of the community, should be constantly evaluated in terms of their worth to the youngsters whom they supposedly serve. A court set up to handle the problems of the young, but hamstrung by lack of ability to see to it that the youngster gets the treatment he or she needs, might as well not be there. No one can hope to break up the "gang" of teen-agers unless he can offer something more valuable to the members of the gang. To leave youngsters in homes that destroy any human decency, to leave unsatisfied their most rudimentary requirements for social life and recreation, for education and inspiration, is to invite them to re-form on the old lines. To set up a system for chasing truants back to school without any supporting system for finding out why they play truant in the first place is an unintelligent way to provide employment to truant officers. It certainly doesn't prevent truancy. To spend community money to be sure that "unfortunate girls" are taken care of during their pregnancies and not give them expert help in understanding their motives is a flagrant disregard of good sense. To support churches that do nothing to attract young people is empty religion.

What we must have is co-ordinated planning. This takes understanding and determination. A community that wants to eradicate delinquency can probably do so, to a large extent. But it will have to spend its treasure and its energies without any picayune considerations. It will start at the beginning and carry through. The community organization for young people should be made up of representatives of every part of community life. There should be a continuing program for spotting the early signs of delinquency and immediately instituting remedial measures. An educational project on a greater scale than that directed toward the discovery and treatment of cancer would have to be set up. Everyone in the community should be made aware that delinquency is no respecter of persons; that it isn't a disgrace unless it is neglected; that it can be treated; that if neglected it will produce more misery than any other plague. A scientific effort to discover all its causes would be a part of any useful enterprise of this sort.

Once trouble was suspected or found, the energies of the whole town would be turned to seeing to it that the youngsters involved had the maximum opportunity to recover and be put back in working order. The idea of punishment would have to be thrown overboard. Beginning with the family (the most likely source of the problem), the whole area in which each one lived and had his being would be studied to find the cause of the difficulty. A careful and thorough scrutiny by experts would yield the answer. Then, instead of remanding the youngsters to the nearest corrective institution, where they would be likely to discover all kinds of refinements of techniques they had only begun to understand, there would be a concerted plan for treatment in every department of their lives that required it. If, for example, parents needed help with their difficulties and their attitudes, facilities would be provided. But direct help to the delinquent himself would be of first importance. And it would have to be given when it was needed. You can't wait until the juvenile has grown into a full-fledged criminal to begin treating his difficulties.

This program would cost money. Indeed it would—but not more than juvenile delinquency and adult crime cost the state today in the care and handling of those who are, and must be, confined over and over again. And that cost does not include the terrible loss of human energy which should be part of the total energy of the society. The prevention of

suffering must also be taken into account. It is worth anything that can be paid for it.

Admittedly this is a Utopian idea, and that is precisely
what recommends it so highly. In a situation as miserably
handled as this one generally is, it would be just as well to
go at it in an over-all way. Tear down the useless old structure and start from scratch. Probably nothing short of that
would work. Obviously it is not possible to build a program of this kind all at once, but there can be a plan which
works toward it. There isn't an adequate supply of well-
trained people to cope with the difficulty, but there can be if
the demand is felt. If we are to believe the screams of the
press, the predicament is certainly serious enough to warrant
Draconian measures. When stories about wild promiscuity
among teen-age boys and girls, murder by the young, car
robberies and hold-ups are daily newspaper fare (as they
are), it is time to start doing something pretty radical
about it.

When the misery and destructiveness of the situation and
the torment and neglect implicit in it are appreciated by
those who now are apparently content to congratulate themselves that their own backyards are clean; when any delinquent youngster is a great challenge to every parent
as if he were that parent's own child and entitled to the same
care, protection, treatment and consideration; then we will
have a beginning to the end of our problem. This is a large
assignment in today's crowded city, where there is no
neighbor and little sense of common identity. When it is a
case of each for himself and the devil take the hindmost,
the devil usually does. He certainly does in the case of these
lost, hopeless, defiant, needful young people whom inner
catastrophe or material deprivation or both have driven into
the desperate role of outcasts. We can stop it when we will.

X

Homosexuality

We are devoting a chapter to the discussion of this unfortunate variation in sexual development because it seems to be increasing. Furthermore, the public is widely aware of it. Until we have further evidence of a more definite nature, we cannot be absolutely certain that the apparent increase is actual; nevertheless, the decided possibility that it is warrants our giving careful consideration to the causes and possible prevention of the condition.

Homosexuality is a retardation of development or an actual deviation from the normal; feelings of love which should be directed toward persons of the opposite sex are directed toward those of the same sex. It may be an open condition or one which is concealed and even unknown to its possessor. Of the two, the concealed or covert type may cause more damage precisely because its possessor is unaware of it and may assume himself or herself to be capable of attachment to a person of the opposite sex. In the first instance there is no confusion possible, since attraction to the opposite sex is almost wholly in abeyance while attraction to the same sex is clearly felt and apparent.

The origin and development of such an abnormal state are extraordinarily complex. The early sexual development of the individual has been already described, but it is necessary to emphasize once again the disordered nature of it. In the beginning, the young infant's sexual drives are toward getting sensual satisfaction from whatever source and in whatever way available. There is no more concern at this time about the person from whom satisfaction is obtained than there is about the nature of that satisfaction. The young human infant has a nervous organization which, roughly speaking, makes its entire body a sexual organ capable of receiving pleasure-inducing stimuli. The mouth, the skin, the muscles, the urinary and anal orifices as well as the genital apparatus can act as areas of potential pleasure. This organization is first centered most intensively in the mouth. In the newborn this insures an impulse to suck and serves the purposes of survival by maintaining nutrition. As development progresses, the various other areas become for a time dominant centers of pleasurable sensation. As the mouth becomes less crucial, the skin, the urinary and anal areas in turn assume a central importance. All are at all times susceptible, the difference is one of primacy. But in the course of these changes, there is a steady tendency for satisfactions from all sources outside of the genital to decrease. While the child still obtains pleasure from all kinds of stimulation, little by little his increased awareness and the organization of the nervous system insure that pleasure is most certain, most direct, and most intense in the genitalia. If one looks at development as a purposeful undertaking, this fact is seen to be of first-class importance. This and this alone insures that the requisite amount of energy is fixed in the genital and therefore available for reproductive purposes. In man, pleasure is an ineradicable part of the reproductive drive.

At one period of growth, there is a natural acceptance of a homosexual object. This is easily seen in the girl child, who is at first dependent upon her mother for all satisfactions. Therefore, strictly speaking, the first love object of every girl is a homosexual one. In the boy this particular aspect of the situation is delayed until he is ready to turn to his father for love and satisfaction. In the case of both boys and girls, of course, the earliest satisfactions are those the mother furnishes in caring for their needs, her care giving pleasure of a sensuous sort. In return, the child learns to give his only gift of love. The loved object is precious and cherished for she means life and pleasure. For both boys and girls, the father too has many ways of satisfying and soon becomes, next to mother, the most valued person. At first, he is loved along with mother. Later, he becomes more important and, in the case of the girl, the desired and preferred object of devotion, looked to for all satisfactions. At the same time, the boy develops the same attitudes toward the mother. With this event, the Oedipus complex is ushered in and the next years are spent in its gradual resolution.

Finally, the child, under the influence of the anxieties that these feelings produce, and for the sake of parental love, gives up his unattainable strivings, but the inevitable disappointments and denials of this solution force the child to seek consolation. This he finds by turning to himself for the satisfactions that are not forthcoming from the parent. He has already discovered the pleasure that can be had from the genital. It is a logical step, then, to find the longed-for pleasure through himself, handling and playing with his genital. He is, as it were, in love with himself and provides himself with pleasure. This will not be permitted by the parents either, to be sure, and will have to be secretly indulged in. Later, it will be put aside until the drives of puberty and adolescence reactivate it.

At so vulnerable a time, the young child is extremely susceptible to any kind of stimulation or exploitation by those around him. He has as yet no inner equipment with which to protect himself and is very strongly disposed to take pleasure wherever it is available. For this reason, seduction by anyone is easy. Many homosexual adults can give a history of having been early seduced by some older person of their own sex. Unfortunately, there are enough homosexual adults to make this a not impossible occurrence.

It is not a trivial matter to be passed over with the comforting notion that the child is too young to be aware of what
is going on. Human beings tend to wish to repeat whatever
gives them pleasure and to avoid what does not. It is no less
so with sexual satisfaction. For this reason, early sexual
stimulation of children by others than themselves is a prime
danger, often serving to keep active the sexual feelings that
the child will otherwise show a disposition to put aside for
the years between seven and twelve. Those feelings can,
however, always be stimulated and activated, and it is
probably true that many children in these years do have
some sexual activity or interest. But, by and large, sexual
concern normally subsides at this time, to provide a period
of quiescence which the child needs in order to strengthen
his personality powers for the struggle to come in adolescence.

There are other situations in childhood which may lay the
foundations for later abnormal sexual development. Circumstances which expose the child to brutalities of a sexual
nature may have a great effect. Exposure to parental intimacies may be dangerous, and should be avoided at all
costs. No child can witness sexual activity without reacting
to it. He will feel that it is a brutal and violent attack by
the male on the female. Inevitably the child's own feelings
will be aroused also, and he will wish to play one or the
other role. It is not unusual under such circumstances for
him to want to play the role of, and have the pleasures he
imagines are those of, the parent of the opposite sex. Frequent or repeated stimulation of this sort may promote the
development toward homosexuality.

Anything in the child's surroundings that makes him see or
feel his role—the role of his own sex—as undesirable, guilty,
bad in any way, can also turn him away from it. The mother
who by her attitude or words, indicates that the man's part
in life is cruel, beastly, burdensome and dirty is communicat-

ing to her sons and daughters a view of life that is vastly alienating. Particularly damaging to the boy is the impression that the father's relation to his mother is painful and repellent to her. His love for his mother may start him in the direction of renouncing such a role for himself.

Another effective way to disturb the smooth sexual development of the child is for a parent to seek excessive love from a child of the opposite sex. This situation is not so uncommon as one could hope. For the most part, the parent is unaware of what he is doing. Quite early and naturally, a man or woman who is disappointed in his spouse may turn unconsciously to a son or daughter for the love and devotion which has seemingly been lost. If this circumstance is present during childhood and is continuous, it is certain to play havoc with the child's sexual development. The child is too weak to oppose the desires which such attitudes arouse in him, but neither can he avoid the feelings of guilt that are also engendered. If the mother or father becomes for the boy or girl the whole expression of sex, then all women or men must be given up as sexual objects. The only path left may be the homosexual one.

Another destructive influence is the determined wish of the parent that the child should be sexually what he is not. The mother who insists upon trying to make her sons into girls may succeed in doing exactly that, as well as the father who is eager to have his daughter be a son. Furthermore, the mother can deprecate her daughter's femininity to the point of its destruction.

It should be (but, alas, often is not) as simple as A B C to understand that the first duty of the parents is to foster and promote the complete acceptance of whatever sex the child may be. The boy's masculinity and girl's femininity alike should be served at every turn, never opposed, never belittled and never threatened. These requirements reach into the smallest detail of the child's life, from dress and personal habits to the toys and play materials with which the child is provided. Electric trains and steam shovels, footballs and bats are boys' toys and have to do with masculine undertakings, and no amount of "modernism" has yet changed that. Furthermore, girls wear skirts and boys wear pants. While for convenience' sake, the little girl may often live to a great extent in overalls, her femininity will nevertheless require that the reason for this be kept clear and that plenty of attention be given to her innate longings for feminine beauty and charm. Pushing this aside as "impractical" or "too much work" can only convince the little girl that her mother has no regard for her feminine attractiveness and does not wish to promote it.

There are still other forces that may operate to similar disastrous ends. Fears of the opposite sex may be aroused through various complex and profoundly unconscious activities. These may involve all sorts of misconceptions about the nature of the body of the opposite sex, which may make the body appear to be a source of danger and destructiveness instead of gratification and completeness. The parents cannot and need not follow all these difficult formulations. It is important for them to be sure of their own roles and to be able to recognize the signs of danger in their children if and as they arise. Some of the symptoms can be seen in childhood. Extreme girlishness and preoccupation with girls' interests in little boys and its reverse in girls should be watched; also excessive attachment to the mother by boys and to the father by girls, if it continues beyond the expected time.

With adolescence comes the expected sexual awakening. Now the sexual feelings are no longer mainly unconscious, but are plainly recognized by the youngster. And as a result of the intensified pressure to find an outlet for his sexual needs, there is a natural tendency to form attachments to those of his own sex. The first sign of this is to be found in the hero worship and so-called "crushes" of early adolescence. Hero worship is directed toward a person of the same sex but one who is much older. A "crush" is developed toward a person of the same age and sex. Both are basically homosexual, but neither should arouse any alarm if they are not too intense, absorbing or prolonged.

A case of hero worship or a "crush" that extends over a long period and shows few signs of breaking up and yielding to a heterosexual attachment usually indicates a strong homosexual disposition. In the hero worship there is always the possibility that the youngster will select as his idol an older person who is himself homosexual, and that a homosexual relationship will be formed. It is also true that older people with homosexual tendencies will select youngsters of this age as objects of their own interest and affection. Parents will have to be reasonably watchful about such things. There is no need for excitement or alarm, but there is definitely need for knowledge and watchfulness. A youngster in his early adolescence is so malleable and so impressionable that he is at the mercy of any and every influence. This of course is the reason for the general rule that the associates of an adolescent child are enormously important in his over-all development; but it is especially true as far as his sexual development is concerned.

Obviously and most unfortunately, the youngsters whose sexuality is uncertain are precisely the ones who may be selected by an adult who is himself abnormal sexually. It is a fact that some adults who select activities which keep them in contact with youngsters do so because they satisfy their unconscious homosexual drives in that way. Then when they are brought into close contact with a boy or girl who is particularly susceptible (perhaps only temporarily), the whole underlying mass of feeling erupts and the youngster is seduced by the older person. This cannot escape being a calamity.

The youngster may have been quite able, to that point, to manage the impulse within himself. He may (and this is very often true) have been expressing it by converting it into the highest and most delicately tender feelings of devotion and loyalty. It is all too plain what is apt to happen when the youngster's hero presents him with such a problem. His own deeply buried desires for precisely what occurred will produce a mountain of guilt. Or if that is not the case, his most delicate feelings will be outraged, and his confidence in the strength and goodness of the adults around him badly shaken. Or his own latent homosexual drives will be so activated and increased that there will no longer be any way of preventing real homosexual activity. A relationship between the two may grow up that will consume all the youngster's vital energy, leaving none to be used in relationships of the opposite type. Young people occasionally allow these relationships to continue for some time before they tell their parents or another adult, precisely because it really pleases them deep down in their unconscious minds. Ultimately, their feelings of guilt may force them into a confidence, but by then much injury may have been done.

It isn't safe to say that these distressing events "caused it all." There was something there to begin with. The author has seen many adults who have given a history of just such early exploitation without such effect on their later sexual development. But that doesn't make it a desirable circumstance, nor does it remove the need for the parents to be aware of the possibilities. The vital point is the extreme delicacy of the child's inner balance at adolescence. It stands to reason that any circumstance that disturbs this delicate adjustment may mobilize and activate all the latent homosexual energies of the child's nature.

Homosexual feelings in an adolescent are not always directed toward an adult. Two youngsters of nearly the same age may as easily be involved in such an affair. Usually, one of them is more aware of his inclinations than is the other, and will take the lead in the relationship. There may be a period of some activity between them, but often the relationship never comes to any explicit expression. There is only an idealized love and devotion of a tender and delicate nature, deathless closeness and loyalty that are not duplicated in any other association. They have a great need for each other, see one another as often as possible, share all experiences and feelings, give to each other in all ways and are bound together with particular closeness.

We must not, however, delude ourselves into believing that it is always so delicate a matter as this. Many relationships are directly and overtly homosexual in their physical expression. They may be prolonged and mark the beginning of a lifetime commitment to abnormal sexuality. Or they may be only transient, soon abandoned for the search for a partner of the opposite sex, and then forgotten. In any case, it is best to have a watchful eye upon a situation as explosive as this kind is apt to be. No sort of head-on attack will discourage it. Criticism or attempts to disparage the object of the youngster's devotion will make matters infinitely worse.

It is well to remember that some of these first homosexual "hero" objects very often represent an attempt to find a substitute for the parent of the same sex. Parents may experience a good deal of jealousy in such situations. Their feeling won't be recognized as jealousy but rather will appear to them as a natural, proper concern for the boy's or girl's welfare. There are a thousand ways a parent can deceive himself about anything as distasteful to him as the idea that he could be jealous of his own child. But the wise and honest parent will, nevertheless, search his mind for that possibility.

A youngster whom the author knew well suddenly disclosed to her mother a fond, even passionate attachment to a woman teacher. The situation became apparent when circumstances suddenly forced the child to face a separation from her. The woman, who was very nearly the mother's age, was the first "great teacher" that the child had met, and was leaving to live a long distance away. The parting was accompanied by tearfulness and expressions of deathless devotion, and for a considerable period the child kept up a constant correspondence with her. The child of course did not recognize that this was the first emergence of her adolescent homosexual drive. Her mother gave the friendship every encouragement as being of an ideal nature, admired the teacher as warmly as was necessary to allay any feelings the child might have had of disloyalty to her, and helped the child to keep in contact with the teacher. There were, for instance, many occasions on which, because of the particular circumstances of the teacher's life, the child could express her love through gifts which were of special value to her. The connection was maintained for some months with apparently an added intensity, but little by little it was easy to observe that the attachment was diminishing; gradually it was converted to a less intense and more reasonable regard without any loss of loyalty or admiration.

This is a happy story, but there are many less happy ones. The author calls to mind the case of a young girl emotionally deprived by reason of the death of her father and the indifference of her mother. Soon after her father's death she formed an attachment to an older adviser who exploited the girl's feeling for sexual reasons. The whole of the girl's ardent nature was aroused and what had been latent became all too obvious. The older woman was none too anxious to continue the relationship, which she herself had been instrumental in establishing, and was finally forced to break it off ruthlessly and cruelly. The young girl responded to this disappointment with all the feeling of betrayal that might be expected in a jilted young lover. But the rupture did not impair nor unseat the drives that had been activated; instead, it made the young girl intensely aware and intensely desirous. For her the result was a wish to find again and in the same way the happiness she had lost.

Fortunately, in most cases early homosexuality is simply a phase of development through which the young person passes, and which leaves no important residues. It is an inevitable part of the development toward fully adult heterosexual love, and its causes are relatively simple. In the first place, it is part of the young person's effort to become an individual in his own right, independent of his parents. And that effort, as we have seen earlier, requires an ideal to strive toward. Usually the child selects an older person who represents the things he would most like to be and have, and identifies himself with his chosen idol. In order to do this, one must love such a person very deeply. Such love usually endows the loved one with perfection, exactly as later adult love tends to do. The youngster sees himself in his hero and in loving his object he loves himself.

The second cause is linked to the first. In the child's need to fight against his drive toward the parent of the opposite sex, to overcome the forbidden incest feelings, he may, for a time, turn away from all persons of the opposite sex. If a boy, he identifies all women with his mother, who is taboo; all women must, therefore, be avoided. These inevitable and natural developments may be re-enforced or exaggerated by some of the early experiences previously described which tend to foster later abnormality.

A number of investigators believe that some persons who develop adult homosexuality are born with a disposition toward it. Where this is true, and if it is true, it will, in all probability, have been evident early in the child's life and long before adolescence. Of course, it becomes much more evident as soon as adolescence is established. Such youngsters often display a decided disinterest in or antipathy toward the usual activities and concerns of their own sex, along with a tendency to identify with the opposite sex. Boys who show a liking for girls' occupations and girls' dress and fail to develop the usual aggressiveness and power can be looked upon with suspicion. The same can be said of girls who are excessively tomboyish, demand boys' clothes, reject all girlish dress and occupations, and wish to associate with boys in play.

These characteristics, to be sure, do not necessarily arise from hereditary causes. They can be brought out by the circumstances of early handling. The mother who sees only manliness as desirable, who greatly admires her son to the disadvantage of her daughter, and who strongly rejects her own feminine nature, is scarcely likely to encourage the development of true femininity in her daughter. Contrariwise, if she wishes her son were a girl, he may begin to show his compliance at adolescence by unmistakable girlishness and a total disregard for what is expected of him as a boy developing into manhood. Sometimes he may even show accompanying feminine physical qualities—softness, grace, delicate voice, gestures and carriage. His counterpart is the girl who minimizes all the feminine contours of her body, exhibits a masculine stride and, over all, tries to give the appearance of mannishness. In these circumstances, particularly if they are persistent, the parents cannot avoid seeing the direction in which the youngster's development is going and will continue to go unless help is provided.

Nothing is more distressing to parents than to find a child developing in this direction. Everything possible should be done to prevent such a catastrophe, to avert it if it seems imminent, or to remedy it if it has developed. Prevention is sovereign here as everywhere. The most important measures will have been taken before the teens are reached, though even in those years care may prevent injury to a susceptible or delicate child. However, most of the work will have been done or not done by that time. Parents who have accepted each other and each his own role are the first requirements, of course. They will welcome the child's sexuality for what it is. And they will not present to their children a distorted or damaging view of the relations between men and women. They will not make excessive demands for love and they will not reject. They will provide the needed green light. At adolescence this kind of help is of even greater importance than before, for this is the child's last chance to accomplish the task of becoming fully mature. Many times the things that young teen-agers will do to assert their growing sexuality will seem to the parents extreme or ridiculously unnecessary. But in order to be very sure of his or her identity as a man or woman, the youngster may have to resort to such emphasis. Everything that the parent can do to support and fortify the child's growing sureness is useful and desirable.

Before discussing the problem of preventing and handling these difficulties, a word of warning. If the explanation that has gone before has the effect of making parents look for the bogeyman of abnormality behind every relationship a child may develop with another of the same sex, it has missed its goal. But to delude oneself that it can't happen to one's own child is just as silly. The desirable middle course is to look straight at the facts without alarm or complacence.

How best can parents prevent such difficulties from arising? First: Know your own children. The best and most effective insurance is a good relationship between the youngster and his parents. If there is mutual love and trust, the child will be able to turn to his parents and tell them of his trouble. But the parents must understand the nature of the difficulty, as far as possible, and accept the fact of its existence. This does not mean that they should complacently watch a youngster plunge into a dangerous situation without lifting a hand. It does mean that they will have to accept homosexuality as a problem, not as an immoral or disgraceful flaw. It is impossible to handle the problem by punishment or hostility, and the surest way to alienate the child and lose any chance to help is to show horror or disgust. It is wise not to respond to the knowledge as if it were a four-alarm fire. Often the situation will take care of itself in the course of time, and what the child needs is frankness and help in understanding himself. Above all, love and trust, not fear and suspicion, should be dominant. It is imperative to make the youngster feel that he cannot lose his parents' devotion no matter what kind of problem he presents. Homosexuality is not a disgrace, not evidence of "bad blood," not a sign of moral turpitude, not the end of everything. It is a sickness; and what is needed is determination to help, not to punish.

Second: Know the associates of your children. Accept them and welcome them as friends of the family. This will give you an opportunity for real judgments, reached on a fair and reasonable basis. It is dangerous to stay outside the boy's or girl's life and so know nothing about it. If certain friends arouse suspicion, it is best to look carefully into the matter and to be sure before jumping to any conclusions. If in doubt, consult someone else; put your suspicions and the evidence to a person who is trained to recognize and understand the signs of homosexuality and who is not emotionally involved.

If, after this is done, there is reason to believe that a homosexual relationship is developing, it is time to act. But your interference must be most carefully gauged not to frighten or anger the youngster. First: Try to break up the friendship by encouraging other associates and activities. This is easier to do, of course, if the business is taken in time, before the relationship has been consolidated and before it has asserted itself openly. If that fails, the situation must be faced openly with the young person himself. Only a firm, but unaccusing and gentle statement of what the parent believes to be true will be of any use. One cannot make vague or generalized passes in the air at this point. Such comments as, "I don't like his (or her) influence; so-and-so isn't the kind of friend for you; the situation doesn't look right to me," will lead exactly nowhere except to hostility and defiance or bitter hurt and disappointment.

Much better the facts: that the young person in question seems to be unsure of his own sexual position; that that seems like a poor thing for both of them; that for that reason one feels it would be better to make a less exclusive business of it, or to discontinue the relationship on such an intense basis. The youngster may welcome your interference even if he blusters about it. He may be furious and vow to commit all sorts of desperate acts if he is required to give up the friendship, but if the parents are sure (as they must be before this kind of move is made), they must stick to their point, only agreeing to talk it over with someone else if the boy or girl can't accept the parental viewpoint.

Third: Get expert help. If, after you have done all you can, the situation still progresses and the young person becomes involved in a real homosexual relation, the only answer is the quickest possible resort to psychiatric help. To try to hide the existence of a homosexual attachment or to deny it from a sense of wounded pride or shame, is cruel, if not criminal, neglect of a situation which threatens the youngster's life happiness. Psychiatric help is the only remedy for this problem. Nothing should be spared to secure it if it is needed. Many of these young people can be helped to live through homosexual experiences without any damage to their later sexual lives, but the earlier help is made available, the greater the chance of success.

Some, necessarily and unhappily, must and will continue to be homosexual. These young people, too, need help, for it is no easy task to be a homosexual person in a heterosexual world. The mere fact of abnormal sexuality does not condemn its possessor to the life of a pariah; it does not mean that he cannot be useful and successful and contribute greatly in all other fields. There have been many greatly gifted contributors to our world who were homosexuals. Leonardo da Vinci, Dostoyevsky, Tchaikowsky are three among very many. But the condition brings with it penalty and misery. A homosexual cannot live the complete life of the normal individual. He must go through his life without the security of love and family. He must often live in loneliness and isolation. No one should be left to such unhappiness unless help for him cannot succeed. If he is forced to accept this condition, he must learn how to live with it without injury to himself and others. Whichever the circumstances, the answer must be found through expert guidance and help.

XI

Psychosis and Neurosis

The previous two chapters have discussed two not uncommon but extremely troublesome variations in the development of young people. They are by no means so common, nor do they take so large a toll in human misery and loss of effectiveness, as do two disturbances of development resulting in emotional and mental illness: psychosis and neurosis.

Psychosis is the rarer of the two as well as the severer, involving all parts of the personality. It is roughly the same as the layman's term "insane." Neurosis is less severe and much more common, involving only a part of the individual's relations to reality. Thus a person who is psychotic is often entirely deranged in his view of the life around him. His social, emotional, intellectual and work life is disrupted. In the case of the neurotic individual, only some parts of his life are disturbed. He may have a great deal of anxiety but still be able to carry on his routine activities. He may have very poor relations with those around him but be most accomplished in his professional life; he may have all sorts of bodily complaints but nevertheless have satisfactory contacts with people. However irritating and maddening his attitudes may be, he will not seem markedly different from others or bizarre. He will not make any mistakes about the facts of his existence. He will not be unable to distinguish between imagination and reality.

A psychotic, for example, may feel that people around

him are antagonistic to him. He will believe this to be a fact and may elaborate it to the point of thinking that he is the object of a widespread conspiracy. His entire mental life may be concerned with this, to him, indubitable reality. The neurotic person may also feel that he is not liked, but he will know that it is only a feeling; he will not believe in its absolute reality and he will not let it govern his entire life. A psychotic may have ideas that are obviously untrue, such as that he is being poisoned or injured by magical means. The neurotic may certainly fear meeting a black cat on his way to work, but he will never believe he is being followed (unless he is).

We will discuss psychosis first because, since it is less common, we can deal with it more briefly. There are many varieties of psychoses, but in connection with adolescence, the principal one is schizophrenia, sometimes known as dementia praecox or "split personality." The word "praecox" (precocious, early) gives the key to this illness and indicates its tendency to make its appearance at this time of life. It is a disorder of great severity, and tends strongly to be chronic. Like any other illness, it yields far more easily to treatment in its earliest stages; consequently, the sooner it is detected the better. It is, by all means, the most common form of severe *mental* illness today and the one responsible for the largest number of hospitalized individuals. Because it may be very subtle and insidious in its onset, the parent may ignore it or neglect it, assuming the changes he observes to be transient or inconsequential. On the other hand, it may begin suddenly and dramatically.

The most conspicuous and often earliest sign that something is radically wrong in the development of the youngster is a growing detachment from his usual interests and concerns. He becomes brooding and secretive, often spends long periods of time by himself, and increasingly avoids associations with others. Very often he is depressed and concerned about himself, appears worried and upset, but declines to share his difficulties with his parents. Interest in social activities and in school begins to fall off. This is particularly noticeable when the school accomplishment has previously been satisfactory or better. Many times the youngster becomes preoccupied with subjects of cosmic or philosophical significance and is overconcerned with his relations to the universe and his position in the world. He grows more and more remote; and his connection with people and events becomes progressively more tenuous. Exaggerated attitudes toward sex—extreme aversion on the one hand or greatly magnified interest and unrestrained activity on the other— may also indicate the beginning of a serious mental illness.

Sometimes these children have very striking mental aberrations; for example, they may begin to believe that their bodies are in some way deformed, or particularly loathsome, unattractive or asymmetrical. These complaints are important, because they may be separated by only a very delicate line from the natural but exaggerated concern about the body that all adolescents display. Parents are therefore apt to dismiss them without realizing their seriousness, on the grounds that "all youngsters feel that way." Often these youngsters are described by their parents or associates as "queer" or "strange," without any more accurate description of the difficulty, because it is so often elusive that they find it hard to put their fingers on any exact abnormality of behavior or of thinking.

In its more exaggerated forms, it is far simpler to recognize the seriousness of the disturbance. There is, for example, no doubt in the mind of anyone that a fifteen-year-old who complains of being followed, spied upon, poisoned or influenced by strange forces is really sick. The trouble is that at this point the illness has progressed so far that it is already more difficult to treat. The earliest signs are the ones that should be watched for, so that the psychosis may be treated when the chances of help are greater. Any disturbance in a young adolescent that corresponds with the symptoms which have been given should receive immediate attention from a qualified expert. Temporizing, hoping for the best, believing that the youngster will "outgrow it," can lead only to disaster. Obviously it is far better to consult a physician and come away without a serious diagnosis than to neglect what may always be a dangerous condition.

The description of a classical situation of this kind may illuminate its characteristics. A girl of fifteen was brought to the psychiatrist after three years of disturbance. By that time her illness was well advanced, but it is easy to see how the early symptoms were disregarded. They began when she was twelve, with a distinct deterioration in her schoolwork, which had previously been distinguished. No amount of urging had the slightest effect. She reported that she was unable to concentrate, and this was a fact. Not long after, she began to show an almost morbid and exclusive interest in clothes. Really fantastic quantities of clothes were provided, but nothing suited her. At one point her mother went so far as to provide her with three separate complete outfits for Easter, only to have her end up wearing the oldest and shabbiest ones she owned. During this time she became more and more convinced that she was completely unacceptable, especially to boys. She began to discontinue her social contacts until by the time the psychiatrist saw her they had been reduced to nothing. She spent every possible minute by herself locked in her room, concerned only and always with her body and her appearance. Her withdrawal finally became almost complete and she began to refuse to go to school, developing meanwhile a fanatical interest in religion. Then she displayed the crucial symptom. She began to complain that her face was asymmetrical, one side being entirely different from the other. She would spend five and six hours looking in the mirror and would try to cover her face when she went out of doors, which was less and less often. She also dropped vague hints that people were talking about her, and looking at her strangely, and was convinced that there was a general, organized conspiracy against her. Finally, she began to have uncontrollable outbursts of rage and tears during which she was incoherent. By this time it was clear to everybody that there was something seriously wrong.

The girl had had a singularly difficult life. Born in another country and orphaned early, she went through a period of gross insecurity when she was placed in institution after institution. Finally she was adopted, but not before much damage had been done. A lonely child without friends or associates, she had turned to herself for consolation. Her problem centered around an unresolved guilt about masturbation. This had started during her infancy at the usual time, but it had not been brought under control. Instead, it continued unabated until the beginning of adolescence, when it became a much more serious problem to her. She was entirely unable to deal with it and unconsciously believed that she had ruined her body, and that the destruction and distortion were obvious to all who saw her. She felt then that she was a pariah and an object of revulsion and loathing to everyone. Unfortunately, her situation had progressed so far that she had to be hospitalized. After long treatment she finally was able to make a partial adjustment outside the hospital.

There are many misapprehensions and misconceptions about the cause of this and other serious mental illnesses. Parents frequently torment themselves unnecessarily by imagining that this or that relatively harmless event in the child's life brought on the trouble, ascribing it to some physical cause, such as a recent severe illness or an early injury which appeared at the time inconsequential—and almost invariably *was* so.

The truth is that the cause of this illness is unknown.

Opinions are somewhat divided. There is a good deal of evidence that the psychotic individual is born with a predisposition toward his psychosis. We cannot say that it is hereditary, but it is becoming increasingly clear that it occurs with more frequency in individuals whose families have had other members similarly afflicted. This is no cause for despair. We cannot say that a child is sure to be psychotic simply because his family has had a large incidence of mental illness. Environment plays a large role and certainly may act to prevent the development of the illness in susceptible individuals—as well as promote it. Some observers believe that a large percentage of people who develop schizophrenia have a history of a particularly injurious relationship with a rejecting mother. However, this is certainly not true of all schizophrenics. The actual sum of our knowledge is that the psychosis is a mysterious, subtle and insidious disease of great destructiveness and severity, undoubtedly arising from a combination of sources both indwelling and environmental.

Treatment is still not satisfactory, although many approaches to it are now available. The kind of treatment to be used depends, to a large extent, on the duration of the illness before treatment is started and its consequent severity at the time that it was first diagnosed. The present, most widely held belief is that every person, and particularly the young, should be given an opportunity to discover whether he can benefit from psychiatric treatment before any of the more radical methods are tried. The final decision about this will have to rest on whether or not the youngster can make a real contact with the person trying to treat him.

Psychiatry probably cannot be used if the illness is of long duration and the individual has completely withdrawn from the world and other people, or if his ideas are particularly bizarre and unreal, or if the degree of disturbance is so great that another person cannot get through to him. For psychotherapy to be useful, the person being treated must be able to recognize, even if dimly, that he has problems; and he must be able to make some sort of connection with another person so that he will be susceptible to that person's efforts to help him. But if the illness is still in its early stages, certainly psychiatric treatment should be tried. It is a tedious and long process, and parents may have to be satisfied with results that are less than they hoped for. But if the individual can be helped by this method, the chances of his making a substantial recovery and being able to live a reasonably comfortable life are probably greater than with any other form of treatment.

However, psychiatric treatment may not prove successful and in spite of all efforts there may be a continuous worsening of the condition. If this happens and the youngster continues to go downhill, some form of shock therapy will probably be recommended. This consists of inducing a convulsion by the use of electricity or drugs—Metrazol or insulin. Usually electric shock is first used and Metrazol is now rather rarely employed. For reasons not fully understood and really only guessed at, a variable number of such "shocks" often gives remarkable relief from troublesome and disabling *symptoms*. The relief will last for a longer or shorter peroid of time but may, and probably will, be followed by a recurrence of the same symptoms, and the course of the shock will have to be repeated. If electric shocks are to be given, it can be done in the office of a psychiatrist who specializes in such treatment. If insulin is to be used, hospital residence will be necessary. In any case, it is probably wiser and more comfortable for both the patient and the family if the patient is put into a hospital where there are facilities for handling the mentally sick.

There is considerable dread about permitting the use of shock treatment, and that dread is easily appreciated. Anything so drastic and so formidable as a treatment that induces a severe enough reaction in the nervous system to bring on a convulsion is rightly held to be a matter for concern. Particularly in the early years of adolescence, there is considerable reluctance about going ahead with shock treatment unless the youngster has been very thoroughly investigated and the possibilities of psychiatric treatment thoroughly exhausted.

There are widely differing views about the use of shock therapies in childhood and adolescence. Some psychiatrists steadfastly oppose any such approach and others recommend its immediate use. The author feels that a middle position is proper. If psychotherapy has been given a good trial and failed, and the course of the illness is downward, electric shock therapy seems indicated. It may relieve many of the symptoms and it may, further, make psychotherapy more effective. Throughout, and at all times, psychotherapy should be pressed wherever and whenever it is possible. If some shock therapy will make it easier to get to the person, when without it he is entirely inaccessible, then such a course is advisable. Insulin may be used to a point short of that necessary to produce a convulsion—so-called subshock insulin therapy. There are occasions when this is effective and, if so, more desirable than the more radical application of the drug. There is no decisive evidence that shock treatment causes any permanent damage to the brain, and there is usually prompt recovery from the passing symptoms of loss of memory and confusion.

There are cases in which all these efforts are useless and appear to have no effect whatever on the steady downhill course of the disease. Under such circumstances, the patient will ultimately have to go to a hospital, where he may improve or where he may remain for many years in a static, hopeless condition. This is admittedly the most tragic and dreaded outcome of this illness, but one cannot ignore the possibility. If the situation becomes that desperate, surgery on the brain may be advised as a last recourse. The procedure is not difficult nor dangerous, but any approach to the brain itself is always regarded as a violent and dramatic operation. The operations vary slightly but, in general, the object is the same: to cut the connections between the forward parts of the brain and the parts farther back. It has the effect of changing the individual's emotional attitudes and greatly lessening their intensity. For example, some psychotics develop the idea that they are being persecuted, or hear disagreeable or terrifying voices. After such an operation (called leucotomy or lobotomy), they may still have the same ideas, hear the same voices, but they won't react to them, and will in fact seem to disregard them.

In spite of all this discouraging information, there are, happily, a large number of psychotic young people who, with help, are able to lead lives approximately like those of most people. The two different possibilities are illustrated by the cases which follow.

A youngster of sixteen was brought by his mother for advice only when he had begun to develop the fantastic suspicion that a number of unknown persons were conspiring to influence him to commit unspeakable crimes. He was a tall, extremely pallid, poorly nourished looking boy who gave the impression of being disturbed and detached. His story brought out the fact that he had first begun to differ sharply from the other children in his family between the ages of twelve and thirteen. He had shown a babyish, clinging attitude toward his mother, rarely wanting her out of his sight. It was only with much persuasion that he had been induced to go to school, where he refused to have any contacts whatever with his schoolmates and kept entirely to himself. In spite of his apparent preoccupation with intellectual subjects, his schoolwork was very poor. He spent many hours by himself, seemingly unoccupied and unable to give any account of what he was doing. Becoming progressively estranged even from his brothers and sisters, he made greater and greater demands for constant attention from his mother. He made no attempt to conceal the fact that he masturbated frequently, freely communicating the fact to his mother. She had been attempting to handle the situation by her care and indulgence for three or four years before she sought help. By that time the boy was entirely out of touch with the world, living in a fantasy of his own making and quite beyond any approach through psychiatric means. This meant that although he was very young, the only recourse was to place him in a hospital, where all the most radical treatments were tried without success.

Another youngster had a happier time of it. She was brought for treatment very soon after her parents observed a subtle, disturbing change in her. She was becoming withdrawn and refusing to have contact with any of her friends. She seemed quite depressed and cried a great deal. When the usual remedies of reassurance and special attention failed, she was promptly brought to a psychiatrist. It was easy to discover in her the earliest beginnings of very severe mental disorder. She felt unreal and remote; she had a kind of "dead" feeling; all the world seemed far away, and she had vague and fleeting ideas that there was something radically wrong with her body. But she was in good contact with the world around her and had a fairly clear realization of the fact that she was in trouble, and she wanted help. It was long and laborious help, but it succeeded in putting her on her feet so that she was able to return to school and social activities and, with careful watching, carry on her normal life.

Happily, the number of children who face this kind of tragic problem is limited. Many more will show difficulties that are less severe but can nevertheless be disturbing and prevent their best realization of themselves. These are the disturbances of emotional development known as neuroses, and they may be either mild or severe. In some degree probably every one shows neurotic trends; it is when the emotional difficulties are of such proportions that the youngster's future development is threatened that account must be taken of them.

Here we shall indicate the symptoms that will come to the parents' attention and which justify an attempt to get help for the child. A youngster who complains of being anxious and fearful for no reason, or for some ascribed reason that clearly is too insignificant to warrant the amount of fearfulness he complains of, is showing early signs of a neurotic development which may plague him in the future. Excessive meticulousness amounting to an obsession; exaggerated cleanliness of the same order; fear of dirt which is obviously not rational; fears of closed or open spaces, subways, the dark, of being alone, of being with people, are all in the same category. Inability to sleep can also be considered a sign of a neurotic problem. Loss of the capacity to concentrate in school, loss of interest in the activities that are of concern to other youngsters of his age, are pointers in the same direction.

Excessive shyness and fear of the opposite sex likewise indicate a difficulty in development which requires help. Any refusal by the boy or girl to accept the natural elements of their sexuality should be investigated. Extreme bookishness, while it may be gratifying to the parent, is often a compensation for a feeling of inability to deal with the realities of life. Extreme and exaggerated resistance to parental discipline, amounting to unmanageability and defiance, is a sign of an emotional disorder and had far best be treated as such than handled as a disciplinary problem. This list may make the reader shake his head and wonder whether he might as well make up his mind that all adolescents have some sort of emotional problem. This is not implied, and the author does not believe it to be true. However, all too many of them do, and that fact must be faced.

Another troublesome sign not uncommonly encountered at this age is the development of psychosomatic illnesses. The reader is aware that it is quite possible for physical illnesses to develop from psychic causes. When an adolescent is extremely prone to illness, or develops a chronic physical disorder for which medical examination yields no real cause, the suspicion is that unconsciously he may be using illness as a way of escape from some insoluble inner problem. Vague complaints centered around the intestinal tract are often of this sort. So too may be allergic difficulties of various kinds. Girls may, and often do, have such problems in relation to their menses. Many times a genuine physical condition is aggravated by the emotional intensity which the youngster channels through the physical illness.

Sometimes a hypochondriacal condition develops. This is a condition in which no relationship can be found between the symptoms of which the patient complains and the condition of that part of the body with which these symptoms are associated. There is no actual disorder in the organ or system, but the person complains nevertheless. In a psychosomatic illness, there is actual disease which is produced by emotional difficulty; in hypochondria there is only the complaint, which is not sustained by any physical defect. Thus an ulcer or constant vomiting are examples of psychosomatic illnesses, while painful menstruation or excessive fatigue or frequent headache or impotence may be hypochodriacal. In hypochondriasis the psyche is using an organ as the medium of expression of a psychic disorder—the organ becomes the pathway.

As an example of a neurotic child, let us look at Tom. He was the oldest child in a family of four, with two sisters and a brother younger than himself. He had always been a delight to his parents, a happy successful boy with a round, expressive face and humorous blue eyes, who had apparently plunged along entirely unconcerned with trouble or worry and looked like fortune's favorite. His parents were therefore understandably amazed when he showed quite marked changes. He began to be quite timid and reluctant to tackle new things, worried about himself and his whole family, became preoccupied with making sure that everything was in order, and generally seemed most unhappy. He even complained that he was "nervous." He slept badly and had some nightmares. These symptoms were not persistent and at times he was comfortable and his old happy self, but they were nevertheless disturbing enough to make his parents wonder and finally take him to someone for advice.

He was by way of developing a neurosis of some proportions. His anxieties were out of all relation to reality, and he knew it. He had many problems centering around his relations to his mother and father which he was more than anxious to ventilate and discuss, and finally learn to understand. Considerably disturbed by the birth of his younger brother and sisters, especially the sister just younger than himself, he had at that time felt neglected and unloved as well as resentful toward his parents, who seemed to him to be abandoning him. They had only done the natural things, but had been unaware of the necessity of giving him particular reassurance. It was especially bad because the little sister was very ill during her first year of life and inevitably claimed the major portion of the parents' attention. His reaction then went unnoticed by the presumably competent nurse who took care of him and succeeded in regulating his naughtiness out of existence. He gradually adjusted to the situation, but when the pressures of adolescence began to be felt, the old problems lighted up and he began to show his symptoms. It was not too hard a task to help him find his way out.

It won't help to attempt to brush aside these difficulties with the comforting notion that the child will outgrow them or that it is perfectly natural for adolescents to act this way. The truth is quite otherwise. These are the earliest signs of a beginning neurosis which may well act as a very disabling factor in adult life. Even though the situation does not appear to be severe, it is well to make the attempt to get some help for the child and not to neglect it. Some of these youngsters can benefit greatly simply by having a counselor who will bring understanding and detachment to the problem and give them support over what may be a hard spot. Others may require more expert aid. Psychologists who have been clinically trained can help with many situations. In most fairly large cities there are a variety of social agencies which provide help with all sorts of family and personal problems. But where the situation is most demanding, where the child is being really injured by his difficulties, is being made progressively less able to deal with his problems and is showing every evidence of failing to develop, a psychiatrist will be needed. And the need for help is urgent and immediate.

Many readers may be disposed to say, "Isn't this making a mountain out of a molehill?" and, "Isn't this business of running to a psychiatrist every time you have a family quarrel reaching ridiculous proportions? Time will take care of it and the youngster will outgrow it."

Time is just as apt to make everything worse as to make everything better. It is foolish to rely on it when what is in question is the youngster's later life. Many times the young person's failure to adjust does not begin to show up until his later school years. He may have carried on up to that point with great success. Everyone has taken his past performance as an index of the future, and is concerned when his forecast is upset. The parents have made all sorts of plans based on their own wishes and what seemed to be the wishes of the youngster. A college has been selected and the longed-for acceptance received. The boy or girl has gone off with everybody's high hopes (except very often his own).

Then comes the catastrophe. His performance is far below what had been expected. Grades fall to unprecedentedly low levels. Failures crop up where only successes were known before. An unsuspected disorganization appears. Headmasters and mistresses find it their unpleasant task to write warning letters to the parents expressing some real doubt about whether the situation can be allowed to go on. Perhaps another school. Perhaps things here aren't quite right for that particular child. College doesn't seem to be quite possible with the competition what it is. Maybe it is better to revise one's plans before it is too late. Principals send for bewildered parents to discuss the child's problems. He (or she) is easily intelligent enough. Tests have shown this but tests are not the final measure. One has to be able to perform. And that is where this particular child seems to fall down. Tutoring may be the thing. Perhaps his difficulty is only temporary, and dropping a few courses and rearranging his curriculum may help. But nothing helps.

Then there will be a transfer to another school where the approach is different and the attitudes more permissive. Still the youngster shows no sign of being able to cope with the situation. The more his environment is molded to his apparent needs, the clearer it seems that no environment is really right, and no sooner have we changed everything to suit the child than we find that the child has changed. Military school is often a choice at this time, especially if a disciplinary problem is linked with the academic, as is so often the case. No need to say that this will end in pure disaster. The boy will find it necessary to violate all the regulations of the school in addition to failing in the school subjects to which he is again exposed.

This situation could be ludicrous if it weren't for the fact the child is having his fortune thrown to the winds by his elders' failure to recognize that all his problems are located within himself and that no shift in the environment will turn the trick. This is true, of course, only where there isn't an outrageous and obvious defect in the environment itself. Bad family relationships or terribly upsetting changes in the child's home life may be important factors in his behavior, and will need investigation if that is so. But even when everyone has done all that they can do, a large number of children simply cannot master their problems by themselves and will have to have expert help at one time or another.

A young girl was brought to the author for advice after she had been asked to leave her fourth school in three years. All the schools admitted that she had superior talents in many directions. Nevertheless, they found themselves unable to manage a situation in which the child literally did almost no work and made no attempt to accomplish the required assignments. Her notebooks were illegible; work was thrown together with deliberate carelessness; examinations were failed with unbelievable regularity; she was insubordinate, violated the simplest rules, and apparently was indifferent to any effort to help her.

All this concealed a state of near desperation which completely denied her outer unconcern. She felt that her parents didn't love her and used school as a way of getting rid of her. A younger brother was much the preferred child and all his accomplishments were praised with extravagant unreality while her equal achievements had been taken for granted. All this aroused a great deal of resentment, and she felt there was no use in doing anything when none of it brought the rewards she so greatly yearned for. Teachers couldn't remove the need for mother love and appreciation. She was finally reduced to a state of sullen defiance and obstinacy, and was unable to work even when she thought she wanted to. Naturally, her failures only added to her feeling of hopelessness. The only help possible for this child was a chance to investigate her inner situation with someone who could understand and give her the kind of aid which would make it possible for her to extricate herself from this vicious circle. It was already late, but she was able to pull out of her despair a determination to find a way for herself and to follow it to the end. She did, and succeeded beyond anyone's hopes in salvaging a very good life out of it all.

Nowhere are neurotic tendencies more easily seen than in the youngster's attempts to cope with the problem of the opposite sex. Their difficulties may find expression either in insistence upon inappropriate association with the opposite sex or in an apparently profound indifference. Every group and every school can produce many examples of both these reactions. Neither is of serious consequence unless it is exaggerated in intensity and very prolonged. A youngster of thirteen who suddenly decides that he or she must undertake all the activities and have all the privileges more properly those of the sixteen-year-old may very promptly respond to controls and reassurance, give up his untimely activities and adopt a more patient attitude toward the whole situation. Obviously, there is no cause for alarm here. However, if his precocious interests persist and fail to yield to reasonable measures, we are faced with a quite different situation, and one that gravely threatens the youngster's educational progress and plans. For many a young person gives up the educational goals he has had because inwardly he is so engrossed with the need to solve the problems of love.

Sometimes sexual problems do not appear until relatively late in adolescence (from eighteen to twenty-three). By then the parents are apt to feel that the period of difficulty is passed and the sailing ahead will be smooth. There is nothing, they will say, premature or inappropriate about sexual activity at this age; it is natural and expected and a hopeful sign. And so it is if the young person's choice of a partner and behavior forwards his achievement of the de-

sired goal. But it is in these years that we often see a variation and distortion of the accepted and suitable ways of
expression. Young people may pursue inappropriate partners. They may enter into a period of uncontrolled promiscuous sexual behavior which brings them repeated disappointment and rejection. They may always fall in love with
people who are unresponsive or who are not available. This
is the case when a youngster is constantly attracted to a
person who is out of reach or so much older that a happy
outcome is not possible; or is attracted to someone who is
already married and only wants to exploit him; or always
forms an attachment to someone who is himself entirely in-
capable of a mature emotional relationship and cannot undertake marriage.

An additional difficulty about these situations is that they
can so easily be rationalized. If the youngster has selected a
partner who is much too old, it soon appears that he is really
not nearly so old as he seems, and that age doesn't actually
count in the long run anyway. If a girl has fallen in love
with a married man, she is likely to be bewitched by the
idea that his present marriage is untenable and cannot last.
Some youngsters will insist that it isn't they who are out of
kilter but the society which sets up such stupid rules. The
boy whose loved one is reluctant or unresponsive will persuade himself that someday, with enough patience and tender treatment, she may be brought around to his point of
view. Whatever the alibi or explanation, this kind of behavior persisted in is a sure indication of some disturbance
within the young person himself.

A girl in this plight finally herself sought help. She was a
talented, handsome youngster of eighteen, who had completed her secondary schooling and then had decided to go
to work, meantime "taking courses at night" at a local university. There she stumbled upon a married man with whom
she very promptly fell in love. She proceeded to carry out

the expected behavior, left home, became his mistress. He was much older than she, successful, brilliant and accomplished, and to her a paragon upon whom she could model herself and whom it was her pleasure to serve. His wife connived with them, taking a casual attitude toward the whole business and even arranging to have the girl a part of the household. The consequences of this were disappointing to her. She not only found no happiness but developed various physical symptoms, seemed never to be well and always excessively tired. Unable to concentrate on her work, she was constantly in hot water with her employer. And she had no friends, since she gave up all her time to making herself available to the beloved man.

She had had a materially secure but emotionally very insecure childhood. Her father had died when she was a baby and after a short time her mother had remarried. Her stepfather was indifferent to her and regarded her as a nuisance while providing her with every material luxury. Her mother took a position of extreme permissiveness, never regulating or controlling anything that the child did. To the mother this passed for love. The child grew up lonely, isolated most of the time and in the care of incompetent and unloving servants. She made little or no social adjustment in school but was sufficiently compliant not to come to the attention of those around her. During her high school years she showed no interest in boys and tended to be intellectual and artistic. Her chance meeting with the man whose mistress she became provided her with a long-wished-for father object, for she had never really known her own father and her stepfather had been no kind of substitute. When she was actually made a part of her lover's household, she was in reality back in the longed-for situation with her father, her mother and herself—before her father's death had destroyed her Eden. Only the facts that the arrangement was so hopelessly and obviously unstable, that she had a great deal of guilt about it, and that she was often ill, brought her to an attempt to solve her difficulties.

Youngsters who pay no attention to the opposite sex are seldom worried about, for they do not appear to be in any real difficulties. Nevertheless these children are often suffering, laying down a pattern, becoming entrenched in an attitude and consolidating a neurosis. Usually they are case histories by the time they are seen by a psychiatrist (the author has seen many adults who have given an account of just such a background), for it is not until the late twenties or thirties that they themselves come to the conclusion that they are suffering from neurotic difficulties and seek treatment.

One such case may be illuminating. A young woman of thirty-five sought treatment because she herself felt that she was not well adjusted, since she had never fallen in love or had any interest in men beyond an impersonal longing. She had grown up in a household in which there were three brothers besides herself. She was the eldest and suffered acutely when her younger brothers were born, feeling progressively more and more neglected. Her mother much preferred her brothers, especially the one next in age to her. The girl plunged into school as a welcome relief, and immediately became an outstanding student and a leader. She and her brothers were nearly inseparable until they were sent off to boarding school and she to a girl's school. She was intensely shy, as well as uninterested in boys, and continued the active physical life which she shared with her brothers and their friends, with never a romantic moment. She early became successful in her chosen profession, in which she worked a great deal with men, and was most congenial and happy with them. Nevertheless, they regarded her more as a companion than as a possible source of romance, because that was the way she wanted it. Gradually, however, she became more and more concerned about herself and finally sought treatment.

There the story was unraveled. She had grown up with a strong feeling that her mother did not want her to be a woman and that there were no rewards for her in it. Her intense attachment to her father and secondarily to her brothers complicated her problem by producing an enormous amount of guilt. In her attempts to solve the problem, she had identified with her brothers and come perilously close to renouncing her femininity altogether.

It is hard to say with any exactness precisely how and when such difficulties are best approached. There are several criteria that may be useful. The first is the youngster's reaction. If he is seriously unhappy and worried, that must be considered sufficient reason to seek expert help. Lack of concern on the child's part, however, is not necessarily evidence that no help is needed; for his apparent indifference may well mask a profound inner disturbance. However, there are very different kinds of unconcern. The unconcern of a youngster who is in no rush to go on to the next stage and new experience in sex, because he is really happy in what he is doing at the moment, is vastly different from that of the youngster who is indifferent to his opportunities to find love because he is indifferent to everything. One is a child who will take things in his stride and simply wants to have a thoroughly digested experience behind him when he goes on to the new. The other is likely to be troubled and unable to tolerate any new experience.

A second test is the nature of the youngster's difficulty. If his behavior shows a striking departure from the generally accepted standards, it probably has a neurotic basis. Are we then to say that any youngster who violates the sexual regulations is neurotic? There is presently so much confusion about standards of sexual behavior that it is particularly difficult to say what is and what is not acceptable. Nevertheless, it is still a fact that the healthy individual will be able to get his satisfactions without too violent an attack on the social norms.

A third and very important test is the matter of duration. The child's difficulty may be merely an expression of some transitory inner anxiety, and in that case will probably disappear as suddenly as it appeared. But when the condition begins to seem chronic, and there is no change in the pattern, it is imperative to accept the fact that it is arising out of unmastered conflicts inside the child himself.

Certainly if all three of these criteria are met, there need be no doubt that a neurosis is in the making. Under such circumstances—or even when there is some uncertainty—it is wisest to act upon the assumption that expert help is needed. Waiting and hoping are notably poor tools in the treatment of any diseased state, and no less when the difficulty is a neurotic one. The parent should feel no shame nor reluctance in frankly seeking advice. The fact is that there are neurotic traits in everyone. The whole question is how much and what kind of damage is the neurosis liable to do? In other words, how severe is it? This is a question that parents cannot hope to answer for themselves. They must have the help of someone able to deal with it, and they may get it from a variety of specially trained people: clinical psychologists, social workers, counselors who are specially equipped, and psychiatrists.

The neurosis should be tackled as soon as it is detected; or at least advice should be sought so that the parent will know what the situation is, where he stands, and what treatment may be needed. Certain factors of development make it difficult to work with children between eleven and fourteen, though even in those years some help can be given. After that, the possibilities in treatment are better. Early help may be worth more than help given when the neurosis has been consolidated by the years. Help that *might not* have been needed will do no harm. But failure to get help when it *is* needed may have unhappy and even serious consequences in adult maladjustment.

The author is well and unhappily aware of the fact that for some readers this advice is tragically ludicrous since no help is available in their vicinities. This is a situation for which parents have to take some responsibility. If the people of a community or a state want services of this kind, the very existence of their wants, if pressed, will eventually make them available. It is imperative for those who need help to have it. If they don't, they are going to suffer from that lack. If they suffer, if they are unable to function effectively, and if they develop destructive and mischievous attitudes toward themselves and others, if they are inhibited from their best and happiest fulfillment, the rest of society will also suffer.

XII

A Program for Parents

By now, the reader is, we hope, familiar with the nature of adolescent development and how it informs and controls behavior. He has seen the many ways in which it can go awry or be influenced in the direction of health or disease. We have shown a chaotic, bewilderingly changing period of life, full of contradictions and excesses. We have tried to expose the forces underlying the enormous surge toward maturity, the problems which are posed for the child as he enters puberty; the demands that are made on him for solution if he is to be successful.

The focal struggle is for a true liberation from old attachments and the establishment of a unique personality capable of self-reliance and self-direction in all the ways of life. The struggle pursues a zigzag course, at times successful and at times flagging. Moreover, the various changes in develop‐ ment do not proceed at an even rate. Physical maturity may be far in advance of intellectual and social maturity, or vice versa. We have pointed out that in society as it is presently organized, dependency is prolonged past the time when sexual maturity would permit mating and reproduction; and we have seen that parents and society seem singularly un‐ decided in dealing with this problem, often saying one thing and doing another.

The adolescent of today emerges from our analysis as largely the victim of the inconsistencies and confusions around him. There is little doubt that, as a group, these

youngsters are not being provided with the kind of environment that would make their development sure and easy.
Somewhere along the line there is mismanagement and failure. Juvenile delinquency and crime are glaring demonstrations of the inability of the youngster to deal with his world,
and the record on that, appalling as it is, does not include
the enormous numbers of youngsters who are not delinquent
only because their misconduct has not come to the attention of the authorities.

But delinquency is by no means the only evidence that we
are not making the grade in the job of helping the adolescent
to arrive at a happy maturity. Less obvious perhaps, but
more important since it involves more children, is the general uneasiness, the lack of confidence between parents and
their teen-age youngsters and the feeling of dismay that the
prospect of adolescence generally inspires. The fact that
parents regard adolescent children as problems—something
to be dealt with—is evidence enough that there is something
wrong between them.

In all that they do, these young people reveal their confusion and aimlessness, and their inability to find in the
adults around them enough purpose, direction and strength
to guide them. They do not seem to know what it is they
want to do or what there is for them to believe in. They
demand all sorts of adult privileges but refuse to accept the
attendant responsibilities. They are great pleasure seekers,
but there is a strong feeling abroad that work is something
that they avoid assiduously. They make excessive demands
of their parents which the parents fulfill helplessly up to the
point where they are unable to comply.

Particularly in regard to sexual behavior the young seem
to have taken matters into their own hands. If we can believe one-half of what is presented as the conclusion of
serious investigation in this field, we will have to dismiss
the idea that the young are doing what used to be known as

"behaving themselves." Having been uniformly brought up and instructed in the belief that they must be sexually controlled and continent until marriage, they often give lip service to this idea themselves. But it is an idea that appears to be considerably more honored in the breach than in the observance.

Parents are dimly aware that this is so, and generally it causes them more concern than any other aspect of their children's behavior, but at the same time they feel themselves helpless to cope with it. They can hope, they can argue, they can bribe, but beyond that they live in perpetual apprehension until the youngster has reached the safe haven of marriage. The worst of it is that usually the parent is the last person to be confided in, for the youngster unconsciously recognizes that his behavior is somehow a defiance of his parents, who have been responsible for passing on the regulation which he is breaking. Once the parents suspect or know that the dreaded catastrophe has occurred, they are in a scarcely better position than before. Doubt is gone; but it is questionable whether the frame of mind induced by certainty is any happier. Furthermore, at that point the parents are forced to take a position and, since they themselves are unsure and bewildered, this requirement is extraordinarily painful.

Probably the most serious evidence that all is not well with our young people is the state of damaged morale with which most of them seem to be afflicted. It shows itself in their inability to take any moral position and stick to it. They often complain that they do not know right from wrong, but there is a very widespread conviction that anything you can get away with is probably all right. The inevitable result of this feeling is an incredible amount of old-fashioned or garden-variety dishonesty. Gypping, cheating, side-stepping, corner-cutting are commonplace and particularly easy to observe in school and college. It is a known fact that colleges today have to maintain an unparalleled vigilance to prevent the whole system of evaluating students' work from becoming a shambles. Naturally, if there is no difficulty in laying hands upon the coming examination, those who can and will pay the price (in money) are going to do better than those who rely on more old-fashioned methods of preparation. Certainly it is far easier to *employ* someone to write a paper on "The Feeling for Nature in Wordsworth" than it is laboriously to haul yourself through the necessary exertions. It is shocking, but there is every reason to believe that this kind of thing is going on, to the horrified but helpless consternation of the authorities, who seem to have no way to stem the tide.

As against this catalogue of disaster there are, of course, many positive elements in the story of the present-day young. Also, we must recognize the tendency of the older generation to believe that "things were different in my day," and to attribute that difference to the greater inherent virtuousness of the individual. If things were different, and they probably were, one factor that almost certainly wasn't responsible for it was any particular natural virtue. Moreover, the young person of today is apt to display one quality that his parents probably did not possess to any such degree; and that is a great eagerness to come to grips with things, to seek out and find the good way, the satisfying life, the productive employment. They want urgently to find out, from somewhere or somebody, what the matter is, why things go wrong, what they ought to do, in fact the answers to all their questions. They are not content to be outside of things, passively accepting whatever is presented to them; they want to find out for themselves.

There probably isn't anything the matter with our young people except what's happened to them since they were born. One often encounters a kind of hostile, critical attitude toward them which could be justified only if they were responsible for the state of affairs in which they find them-selves. No reasonable point of view can possibly embrace the idea that these youngsters are causing themselves and others all kinds of trouble because of any natural viciousness or through any choice of their own. The trouble with much present-day thinking about these things is that it attempts to go in two directions at once. The conviction that all unhap-piness, misbehavior, and failure arises from a failure of moral strength is at war with the conception of the personality as a product of the environment in which the individual was reared. The result is that we often regard a disturbed and disturbing youngster as intrinsically "bad," but lug him off to the psychiatrist or the Child Guidance Bureau to be made "good." This is double vision gone mad. Obviously, the child either is "bad" and needs punishment and reformation or he is a disturbed personality and needs treatment for that disturbance.

Still another popular sentiment holds that all the difficul-ties of the young are due to the misbehavior of the parents who, in this formula, are the villains. This is an extraordi-narily soothing point of view, because it provides everybody with a scapegoat. Presumably, if you have found the villain, the mystery is solved and you can turn off the light and go to sleep. Beating parents over the head from platform and pulpit and in the popular media of expression has become practically a national pastime. The drawback to this "solu-tion" is that it does not go far enough and does not solve the problem. If parents are to blame, then something ought to be done about the parents. If they are not, we cannot mark the case closed but will have to continue to search for a solution.

The truth is that parents too are affected by the temper of their time; they too have backgrounds of their own and have grown up to be what they are through circumstances beyond their control. If this line of thought is followed to

its logical conclusion, we must inevitably arrive, going backward generation by generation, at the primordial ooze. Once
there, we are no better off. Parents do make an enormous
number of mistakes. But a good many of them are hard-
working citizens who believe themselves to have the welfare
of their youngsters as a first consideration. Naturally, what
they believe about themselves and what is true may be two
very different things. But we cannot expect people to operate on the basis of what they do not know and do not understand. For example, a mother who believes that she has
always been utterly devoted to her children and who has,
in her mind, demonstrated this by her unfaltering attention
and care, may, indeed, be jealous of her daughter and be
exploiting her son for her own inner purpose. Under those
circumstances, she is not going to be a truly effective parent.
But she is scarcely an ogre, only a misguided and confused
human being. Similarly, the man who really never wanted to
grow up and unconsciously sought a mother in his wife is
not apt to be the model father on which sons can safely
rely. But this does not mean that he will not make a conscientious attempt to fulfill the requirements as they are
presented to him and as far as he is able to understand them.

And that brings us to another factor that makes parenthood a difficult business today: the insistent and frequently
contradictory advice of the experts. The experts are themselves not in agreement and, it will have to be admitted, are
prone to change their minds. They are numerous and they
represent many points of view. They include educators, police officials, the clergy and the psychological galaxy. Each
group is inclined to believe that it has a grasp of the original
revelation and that if parents would heed its advice there
would be no more need to worry. All groups are equally of-
fenders in this respect, and the beleaguered parent earns
our sympathy in his attempts to sort out their various demands.

The educators have been particularly certain that they have the answer. One gets the feeling that they regard parents as their natural enemies and are convinced that all would be well with the young if the old system of parenthood would only be eradicated. With only a slight effort, one can see troops of bewildered and humble parents passing before their stern accusers, apologizing for their very existence. Some rather bolder spirits among the parents have suggested that if teachers were faced with a twenty-four-hour problem, they might not find it so easy. The clergy is bound to the position that the entire deplorable situation arises from lack of attention to religious life and religious principles, while police officials are apt to have the "big stick" attitude, although lately it is to be noted with pleasure that they are appearing in safety songs and schoolroom mythology as the friends and protectors of the child and the adolescent.

The psychological brethren (of whom the author is one) have various viewpoints, and there is no question but that to some extent they have been responsible for the present parent-baiting. But that was a secondary effect of an attempt to throw some light on a vexed problem. The difficulty has been that the psychological sciences and the theories of dynamic psychology are not final and settled. They change, as all inquiring scientific disciplines must change if they are to remain alive and productive. The changes have been rapid, and many times the public has been induced to accept and to act upon the most recent point of view as final, only to find that it has once again undergone alteration. It was quite possible in late years for the advice of the psychological experts to change almost as often as another child was born into the family. Many a mother brought up her first child in strict accordance with the "books," only to discover that her ideas were completely outmoded by the time the second child came along. In a matter of twenty years the attitudes toward bringing up children have changed from a requirement to abide by an absolutely rigid routine to a demand for almost equally absolute permissiveness. Since these two schools of thought are diametrically opposed, one can hardly wonder if parents find themselves confused and doubtful about the wisdom of all this and, worn out with the struggle to keep up with the experts, decide to give it all up as a bad business and follow their own intuition.

But if parents have been at the mercy of the experts, they have also been at the mercy of much more far-reaching forces, which have operated in such a way as to make the development of a comfortable, well-adjusted personality extremely difficult. It has been particularly hard for women to make the adjustment to their changing circumstances. Their role has been seriously threatened by the developments of industrialization and urbanization, which have made it progressively more difficult for them to find adequate satisfaction in being wife, mother and homemaker. That women in large numbers have been disaffected and made resentful has had no helpful effect on their children. Children are the center of the woman's life and in a sense symbolize the demands made of her. Often she feels that these demands carry with them denials and deprivations, and, where that is so, rejects the children along with the deprivations. Threatened in her feeling of self-esteem, woman has, in effect, deserted the home for the supposedly more rewarding and exciting life of rivalry with men. Or if she has held herself sternly to the performance of what she thought was her duty, she may have become resentful, chafing under the restrictions that children place upon her. The net result has not been any betterment in the relations between children and parents.

It must be remembered that the change in their circumstances was not deliberately wrought, and that women's response has not been studied and planned, but has been the natural, unhappy consequence of forces over which no group in society has had any control. When Watt discovered condensation of steam in his mother's tea kettle, he certainly did not have in mind the revolutionizing of the social order, the erection of an immense industrial machine which would entirely change the face of the earth. Nor until recently did anyone else who arrived at the discovery point in scientific inquiry ever foresee the full consequences of his discovery. Like Topsy, industrialization "just growed" until it reached the point where we now see it. And what in its growth it has done to the position of women and the structure of the family presents us with a problem we have not yet solved.

We may be forced, if we follow these lines of thought, to the conclusion that the entire difficulty in which young people find themselves today is the result of a vague all-pervasive situation which can be called "culture" or the "social situation." Such a conclusion would in all probability be true, as true as it is about any problem that we are required to meet —slums, unemployment, business cycles, wars. Once having found this out, we are no further along unless we divide this "social situation" into its elements and find out where the major stress is felt and what the useful approaches to a solution would be.

There are, however, two pitfalls to be avoided: One is the assumption that since our present situation is a consequence of natural forces, it will have to be left for other natural forces to deal with. The second is the idea that we can go on endlessly working at the surface, patching here and mending there, and never getting at the fundamental problem. On the basis of the first assumption, there is nothing that man can do beyond sitting by helplessly while circumstances evolve to damage or benefit him. It has, of course, been impossible to act on this assumption consistently, for our problems have been too urgent and too numerous to be thus neglected. But when we examine the remedies that have been proposed for the various social ills, we are struck by the fact that they are invariably superficial and treat the symptoms rather than the disease. When, for example, slums and impossible overcrowding demanded attention, we went at the problem by setting up some open spaces, designating "play streets," turning on hydrants in hot weather and occasionally letting people sleep in parks. Getting down to the brass tacks of planning a city so that people could live in it without physical and emotional ruin was quite another matter, and even today there is much more talk than action.

Crime has always been a part of social life and from time immemorial has been dealt with by the method of punishment, in the hope of producing a sufficiently unpleasant impression on the offender to prevent him from repeating his offense. This has been one of the least successful of man's enterprises, having had less than no effect as a deterrent. When delinquency (which is only crime in its infancy) became a recognized problem, we started out by applying the same old formula. Now we are inclined to take a more realistic view and consequently make a greater attempt to "rehabilitate" the young offender than was ever the case with the older one. Nevertheless, our methods have a strange similarity. We try to "take these youngsters off the streets" before we know why they are on the streets. Our major effort is directed at tackling the problem as it first arises, that is when the child is first caught in a delinquent act, rather than at discovering—and thus possibly preventing—the factors that cause it to arise.

It is true that through investigation, study and research, we have learned much about the forces that affect people adversely, especially the young, and much about the pressures under which people are liable to collapse. But the various fields of knowledge have not been integrated or correlated and many times they seem to be pursued for the sake of the pursuit. So, though often the facts are available, we do not use them sufficiently nor disseminate them widely enough to make them really effective. But this must be done if we are, effectively, to solve the problems with which we are faced.

Our attack on the situation cannot be confined to a single point in the wide array of influences to which the youngster is exposed. The family alone (even if it could be regarded as ever operating alone) cannot effect the whole cure. It is the first line of defense, but it is itself immensely influenced by all other forces in society. The schools cannot, single-handed, protect the boys and girls from the deteriorating and destructive forces around them. The remedial agencies that now attempt to cope with the grossest forms of mal-adaptation are essentially only first-aid stations or hospitals whose function is to repair the damage inflicted elsewhere. Churches and religious organizations have demonstrated that by themselves they offer no effective opposition to the disorganization which besets us. The wider community is clearly not geared to give to growing young people the support, influence and example that would help them to achieve a reasonable and wholesome maturity. None alone but all together could accomplish much. But since it is in the family that the impact of adolescence is first felt, it is to the family that society must look and in a wide and co-ordinated effort extend every help.

If, then, as we insist, the individual family is the first source of good or ill for the youngster, it becomes the primary duty of parents to see to it that the family can discharge its responsibility to its members. This will necessitate some conspicuous revision of family attitudes: 1) Parents will have to learn to understand the personalities of their youngsters better. 2) They will have to demand from them greater responsibility. 3) They will have to be willing to exercise greater authority and supply more strength.

If parents wish to understand their adolescent children, they will have to understand them from the beginning, as infants, as toddlers, as schoolchildren. To do this, they must enter more deeply and consistently into their children's lives, be much more a part of everything that touches them, and be a lot less willing to let organized setups take over their problems. The task of being a good parent today is so complex and difficult that it can no longer be left to chance or to the supposed innate equipment of the individual mother or father. That innate equipment is very often confined to the biological—the simple ability to conceive and bear a child which man shares with all other living tissue. We have all along insisted upon the need for instruction and training in the job of parenthood; we insist upon it again here. Ideally, training should begin at the earliest moment of the individual's life, for in some measure all of life is a preparation for this particular job. But for today's parents, who have not had this training and who need help now, we must begin where we can. And that means here and now.

Not all the essentials of parenthood can be taught—proper feelings, for example—but there is a wide area in which ignorance alone is at the root of enormous damage. Many a parent with the best will in the world is unable to do a good job of child-rearing because he is utterly befuddled by all the contradictory advice that is hurled at him. From every side he hears about sex education; spanking vs. no spanking; interference with the youngster's wishes vs. absolute freedom; chores vs. no chores; nights out vs. no nights out; the proper age for dating; the right time for this and that; whether to let junior drive the car or not, and if so when and under what circumstances; is it best to offer the young cocktails at home or will that lead to all sorts of excesses; what children should be given in the way of money; should it be doled out dime by dime or given in large sums for which they must be responsible; what is the right attitude to take toward the young one who refuses to do a thing toward helping in his home or with the parents' burdens; how much freedom should be permitted between the sexes; when should youngsters marry—before they are able to support themselves or not?

Any parent can add to this list many times over. Few feel certain of their stand on any of these points. Fewer still have any real understanding of what it is that makes a young person tick. Yet this knowledge should be part of every parent's equipment. Some will object that it is a matter for experts. To this we can only answer, "Nonsense." It is a matter for parents who wish to bring to their hardest and most rewarding task as much enlightenment and mastery as they would to the economic task. People can learn if there are people who will take the trouble to teach them, honestly and straightforwardly. Everyone can learn at his own level. A college education is not the only criterion of an ability to learn and make use of learning. All sorts of people with all sorts of backgrounds can and will take advantage of an opportunity to find out how to go about their business of living. And no one should fool himself into thinking that the college-educated are not as much in need of instruction as their supposedly less fortunate fellow citizens. Nothing can equal the abysmal ignorance of many (one is tempted to say most) college graduates about bringing up children. They are having just as much trouble as anybody else.

Training for parenthood should be given everywhere throughout the school system as well as in the home. High schools are particularly important in this program, since so many boys and girls don't go on to college. Colleges have been notably derelict in this matter, though in some women's colleges courses in marriage and family life are now available.

A secondary but by no means inconsiderable gain from such a program is to be found in the fact that training for any occupation confers a dignity and value upon it which is inestimable. So it would be with parenthood. The very fact that society regarded family life and child-rearing as warranting the attention of education all along the line would make it a serious matter. Furthermore, everyone would know and understand from the beginning that the business of being a parent was expected of him and that he was responsible for bringing to it the best effort of which he was capable. For girls, it would do much to eradicate the dangerously absurd notion that there was something undignified and unworthy about their most taxing and urgent task. For boys, it would help to instil the idea that they too have an enormous part to play in family life, apart from the business of earning a living.

The author is aware that these considerations are receiving steadily wider acceptance, even if not nearly wide enough. This is, of course, explicit evidence of the obviousness of the need. The peculiar predicament in which family and parenthood were felt to be was the impetus to the calling of the first National Conference on Family Life in 1948. There is an increasing demand for help in these areas and that demand is being recognized ever more widely by governments. There are now specialists in the field of family life. The Federal Government has been active and pioneering in some areas of this vital undertaking. Through departments of health and welfare education, many states have made available facilities designed to assist in the building of such services. For a relatively long time, there has been recognized the specialty of home economics and it has been regularly part of public school curricula. However, this has been much more concerned with the material aspects of home care and management along with the care of children. Latterly, there has been a tendency to expand the viewpoint taken in such courses to consider some of the inner necessities of family and children.

Private agencies also show a growing concern, especially

schools and colleges. In very many of them there are courses of varying types in marriage and family living. Very many of these courses are academic and historical in their emphasis, consistent with the general tone of college curricula. Some are geared to the practical. They are not usually required nor are they regularly integrated into the whole course of all students. Some are part of the study of psychology; others stem from the sociological department; still others seem to belong to anthropology. As indeed they do. Together they make up a sturdy core of study and interest in a vital area. In the lower grades of education, there has, as yet, appeared no way to bring this particular part of life into the child's view. Naturally, this is exactly the time when such aspects of life are especially in the purview of each individual family. It is precisely here that the foundations are laid (or not laid) for a steady and even development into a later, sure adult, convinced of and integrated into his own sexuality. The educational facilities are designed to help parents accomplish just that.

In addition to the formal arrangements of which we have given only a skeletal picture, there are everywhere counseling and guidance possibilities in private agencies of all sorts. The churches take a lively interest in such problems and are increasing their activities steadily. All sorts of family agencies, in the general area of family welfare, devote time and effort to these problems. The organization of marriage counselors indicates by its name its direct and exclusive preoccupation with the difficulties in which many married people find themselves. Mental hygiene associations are more and more spreading their influence and bring more and more advice to those who are interested. Women's organizations are constantly seeking instruction and getting the help for their members of the various experts these organizations are able to provide.

These are comforting and helpful signs. They point, inescapably, to the very wide concern there is about the problems of family living today. There is a beginning but there must be a steady extension and a deepening of these influences from every direction to meet what seems to be a need that isn't lessening but is growing all the time. It is relevant to point out that the impetus for all such activity, as always, has come from a difficulty, a dismay at the problems and disturbances which beset the family today.

We come now to the second point: the importance of demanding more responsibility from the young. The difficulty with the present tendency to let youngsters "enjoy their youth" is that they are not then prepared for the inescapable demands and difficulties of adult life. Anyone who gives a young person the idea that he can take possession of anything he wants or do anything he wants without having to take the consequences is guilty of corrupting the morals of a minor. In the end the young are often profoundly ungrateful for such treatment. The plain truth of it is that no one should be permitted any privileges for which he will not accept responsibility up to his capacity. That applies to everything, even to the small happenings of daily life. And parents should see to it that the tariff is collected. Suppose, for example, the young people decide upon the need for some entertainment—a picnic or a party, perhaps. It is going to mean a lot of work, but plenty of parents will fall in with the idea that all the work will be turned in by the parents and that the youngsters need contribute nothing. The parent is liable to end up with a headache and a sense of resentment, but still defending the notion on the grounds that "it is easier to do it myself than to get them to do it." That point is one of the greatest importance and logically falls under Point 3.

Money is another matter about which vast irresponsibility is often permitted. A good many teen-agers have the comfortable notion that they should be able to call on their parents for an inexhaustible supply of money without having to account for it and without being limited by the most rudimentary common sense requirements. Their only problem about getting it is the proper organization of their tactics. The correct moment to approach father, the delicate evaluation of his mood and the arrangement of one's arguments, is a matter for deep thought. Many parents bribe their young unmercifully. So much money for so much achievement. You would gather that the youngster was doing the parent a great favor by going to college instead of the parent's doing the youngster a service by sending him there. It should be obvious to anyone who has passed the sixth grade that college is an opportunity to which the adolescent must live up, or forfeit the opportunity. As for paying him, it is like paying a child to take a ride on the merry-go-round—and don't think there aren't parents who won't do that too.

Day by day, training must bring home to young people that there are some rules; that the society they live in isn't set up only to render them services but to derive benefits from their creativity; that they have duties that they cannot be excused from; that only responsibility brings privilege. One doesn't expect that more will be asked than the youngster's powers enable him to cope with, but with equal force one cannot expect that less will be asked. It is this business of asking nothing and giving everything that is having such a vicious effect on our young people. To stop it will take courage and determination; but parents must stop it if they want to help their children to grow up to responsible adult life.

The third point of the suggested program requires that parents themselves assume more authority and responsibility, and provide greater support where it is needed. Part, and a large part, of the difficulties of adolescence occurs because it is easier for parents to let responsibility go by the board and simply turn the whole business over to the young.

Right here we may as well state that when it comes to taking responsibility we mean exactly what we say. Parents will have to learn to take over the management of the lives of their teen-age boys and girls where and when there is a need for it. The current notion that youngsters can make all decisions for themselves and that uncurbed freedom is their right from birth on is nonsense and leads straight to anarchy or chaos or license, whichever you like least. Nobody has such freedom and nobody can have it in a social organization. This idea is a noble cover for neglect, indifference, unconcern, lack of love, fear and irresponsibility. It is asking too much of inexperience, and it is depriving the child of one of his rights: the right to have parents who care for him and will give him support and guidance. Adolescents need their parents' strength. They may (and often do) deny this vigorously but, deep within, they are grateful for the parent who can and will say, "No." It gives them something to lean on. It also gives them a source of values. If parents cannot or will not take a moral position, the youngster is hard put to it to know where he stands and what is right or wrong. He needs his parents to set the standards, to light the way, to give him courage, and to take the responsibility when necessary. He needs to be spared some of the big decisions until he is able to make them with more assurance, on a sounder basis.

Many parents complain that their youngsters turn to them only when they want something. They use the home only as a base of operations. They are there only to sleep. Home is only a bank where they come to get money. Why don't they ever stay at home and talk to their parents? Why don't they indeed? Because there isn't anything to talk about. The parents have so thoroughly separated themselves from their young people that neither has anything to say to the other. If parents will make themselves really available to the youngsters, there won't be any trouble about their staying at home to talk. Young people enjoy the companionship of their elders if they find any sympathy and understanding. But the real point is that the purpose of parents is to be there when they are needed, to stand by for the S O S.

This applies in all sorts of ways. The young person may be as greatly in need of parental support and encouragement to go ahead and dare to do and accomplish as he is of the parental injunction not to do. There is a good deal more to parenthood than simply having youngsters who cause no trouble. They may avoid causing trouble by the simple device of causing nothing at all, of being almost inactive and not doing or creating anything for themselves or in their own lives. Or their very compliance may be a cloak for a great deal of fear and self-distrust. To combat this, the youngster may need to draw on his parents' strength. The social situation, for example, may prove threatening to the young and inexperienced, and the timid youngster may be left behind and suffer wretchedly for want of parental help. Some children need regular encouragement, direction and advice to get them on their way to a comfortable social adjustment. Parents are justified in being pretty suspicious of a sixteen-year-old who is happier at home with his father and mother. It may be flattering to the parents but it is certainly far from reassuring. In many other areas a child may be held back by lack of confidence. Work may frighten him; school may be too difficult. Many a plodder became one because he lacked the courage and self-assurance to be anything else. In all these situations parents must give positive and understanding support.

It is, however, the negative aspect of their job that parents more often shy away from. They are reluctant to impose some unwelcome regulation or to deprive the boy or girl of some longed-for privilege partly for fear of courting the child's ill will and partly because it means trouble. Sometimes parents simply acknowledge defeat. "We can't make her do it, he won't do it" are common complaints. This usually means, "I don't want to take the trouble and go through the difficulty of seeing to it that it is done."

This is not the beginning of a preachment in favor of garrets or of throwing the young out to fend for themselves. Nor for a process of "hardening." It is an assertion that extreme permissiveness and indulgence is a form of neglect under whatever guise it appears, and arises from motives which are not apparent to the parents themselves. It is a part of the climate, and a part of the climate which very badly wants changing. It leaves the young rudderless in a sea of indecision and without any guide to reality. It makes them prey to all their own uncertainties. It deprives them of the solid support of the very people from whom they have a right to expect it. It arouses in them not the gratitude and the sense of responsibility that is expected, but cynicism and a disregard for principle. It cheats them of their chance to find out what reality is and to adjust to it gradually. Under such treatment, they will become simply dependent exploiters, out to get from their environment anything they can successfully squeeze from it. Their only standard of value will be: What I want is good and what I don't want or what doesn't pleasure me isn't any good.

Again I must emphasize that to change this corrosive situation will require a great deal in time and devotion and attention and self-denial from the parents themselves. It will require thorough and painful self-definition, for if one has no standards of one's own, one will have an uncommonly rough time of it trying to give them to a young person of the critical and searching nature of the adolescent. A parent who cannot define his own beliefs or convictions can scarcely hope to support them with any strength or determination for and with an adolescent, who by definition is driven to push against restraint or regulation. A man or woman who would rather be consistently popular with his children than uniformly useful to them will never take the trouble to shove his way through the rough going that denial and discipline will undoubtedly entail. Those who must "keep up with the Joneses" will find it difficult to refuse their children anything that other children have. And, finally, those who cannot care enough to place the actual and ultimate success of their young people ahead of their own comfort will certainly never court the ructions that are sure to occur if they put themselves in the way of the single-minded drive for satisfaction that these youngsters can show from time to time.

But the craven are ill-prepared to be parents; and we have perhaps too many craven parents, unable to face not only the disapproval of their youngsters but their own complex feelings. These feelings are so varied that they are found in almost infinite combinations. Those who still cling to their own adolescence will not want to see adolescence deprived of the privileges which they felt they didn't have. Others who are envious of the adolescent will be determined to see that no one (including their own children) gets anything they didn't have. In this, some will go to remarkable lengths. Mothers will rival daughters: fathers will refuse to allow sons any freedom. Then there are parents who are too indifferent to take an interest in anything, so long as their young do not trouble them. Peace at any price is their motto. There is also the parent who likes to use his child as a vehicle for showing off his own power. And for some people, nothing but themselves and their own needs will ever matter when it comes to the pinch.

However, it should be remembered that parents are people trying to do a difficult job and weave their way through a number of vexing and confusing situations. For each family to tackle this task entirely by itself seems to the author absurd. But it is rare to find families making any effort to pool their knowledge, their assets, their common problems and difficulties and to work together toward a common end.

The time is long overdue for some undertaking of this sort. The author suggests that parents living in the same general area should make an organized effort to form a group for the purpose of pooling experience and trying to arrive at a point of view that all can share. If this were done, the interests and needs as well as the problems of the group would become a common concern.

These groups would logically be the building blocks of an organization that could correlate a great deal of community effort. Most small areas in cities contain a group of people who are fairly similar, and who may be brought together in many ways. Living in the same general social and economic area, they are sure to have some common interests and probably some of the same problems. They have the same schools, good or bad, the same cops who are a help or a nuisance, the same traffic to cope with. They go to the same hospital when they are sick, and many of them will have the same doctor; they live in the same kind of apartment owned by the same landlords, and therefore they have the same landlord problems. They must use the same parks or play areas and have the same supervision or lack of it; they have the same hazards in a physical way; they may even have the same kind of jobs and incomes in the same bracket. They may well have similar backgrounds and the same education in general. They go to the same churches and the same bars and taverns. On this basis, it ought to be easy to organize a group that in any case should be small enough to function as a town-meeting type of organization.

A beginning in this direction has been made in Parent-Teacher Associations, which are doing yeoman service in many parts of the country. But the purpose of the groups must be extended to take in more than school concerns. They must be made the heart of an over-all community effort, and as such could easily become the center of very important decisions. Everything that is of interest to, and affects the welfare and happiness of, that small community —the recreational facilities, for instance—could be brought up for discussion. What is most important, such a group could serve as a forum where all the parents of a given part of a city or town could get together to talk over their interests and problems as parents. They would soon find that their youngsters were very much alike, and in discussion could come to a common solution that would lessen the problems of each alone. Attitudes toward certain difficulties could be thrashed out and ways of dealing with definite situations agreed upon. For example, the question of hours and forms of recreation and the amount of liberty to be permitted might easily be made less of an individual family matter and more one for group decision.

This form of organization would have many advantages besides its use as a public forum. It would serve as the basic unit for various community projects. Adult education, whether concerned with child training, politics, economics or social work, would have in such a group a ready audience. Parents could get help and counsel from experts in all sorts of fields, and often those experts might be found in the group itself. If not, the community would be able to supply them. Courses in child development covering the years from infancy through adolescence would be useful. Delinquency and its causes and possible prevention is another subject which could be valuable to parents of youngsters nearing the "dangerous age." A discussion of the meaning and history of the family and of the problems of family life would be helpful to many young people about to marry or in the early years of marriage. A job clinic might well be of very practical value.

The fact that the organization would be set up on the basis of very small subdivisions of the community would make for easy coming together and for flexibility, and would give each member of the group a chance to express himself.

Often organizations formed in part for such purposes as this are too big; they become top-heavy, and finally nothing is left but a lecture platform from which one is talked to about things that have no immediate meaning. To duplicate such programs would be worse than pointless. What is wanted is a natural, almost organic grouping of people with common interests, whose purpose is to help themselves and each other find the answers to their common problems. They would need the services of specially trained people, and they would need someone who could handle the job of starting the organization. But, beyond that, the group would be self-operated and would seek its own solutions with the help which was available or could be made so.

There could be many such organizations in a city of any size, and they would inevitably coalesce into larger groups for those projects which needed the larger effort. A playground might quite possibly be too big a project for the community to undertake for a single neighborhood, but several neighborhood groups acting together might well swing enough weight in numbers to get such a facility placed where it would serve all. Anything that concerned all the groups and, therefore, the whole community would logically be considered by representatives of the individual groups. Thus a central committee for planning would probably be wise and even necessary, but it should never be allowed to become a central control group. It would be better to let a group flounder and struggle for existence than to have it lose its meaning and identity in being taken over by a top committee. For the essence of this program is the fact that it introduces into city living some of the valuable elements of small town life with its closely knit neighborhoods and greater unity. Solidarity becomes a fact. People are drawn together and live as neighbors instead of as strangers, with all the gain that comes from such association. The family horizon is enlarged to take in the small community, and the strength of the community is shared by the families.

Any such plan, if tried, would find plenty of critics. There would be the defeatists for whom nothing can succeed. There would be those who insist that they can never join anything because they have to do their own thinking or because they simply aren't that type. There would be those who objected on the grounds that the idea interfered with the sanctity of the home and its authority. There would be some who would be afraid to submit their ideas and their difficulties to a common discussion. There would be the indifferent and the hostile for whom no plan and no effort ever has meaning. Some would object that the group would only meet the same fate as all others; it would be taken over by people who wanted to use it for their own purposes.

Every one of these objections can be met in a variety of ways. The reality that has to be faced is that we cannot continue to rely on the old supposedly "tried and true" methods of helping the young to grow up. Some sort of daring is needed. The job has to be undertaken by those involved—the parents themselves. Community effort is the answer: efforts right in the community itself, not projects sponsored by outsiders. This is no proposal for more settlement houses or a multiplication of any of the numerous useful and necessary agencies we now have. They are doing, and will go right on doing, their jobs, but they obviously aren't enough. A program like this, if it steers clear of the hazards of formalization and bigness, can be a living platform for people of like minds who want to tackle together a job that involves them all.

Next to the home in influence upon the lives of young people is the school. It is here that they spend the major part of their time. It is here too that they make their contacts with the world of ideas and acquire the skills that they will use in their work lives. The schools have the most enviable opportunity possible to exert a strengthening and invigorating influence, but it is doubtful whether, except in rare instances, they are able to take advantage of their opportunity.

The reason for this, fundamentally, is that the schools are only as good as the citizens of the community want them to be. Any neighborhood that has a bad school has itself to blame and nobody else. Of course, any institution as big and inevitably as routinized as is the school system of a large city falls easily into bad habits. Nor is it a simple matter to find the kind of teachers one would like to have. Nevertheless, in all its parts and ways, a school reflects the attitudes of the parents whose children attend it. Whether apathetic or interested, bigoted or tolerant, spreading conflict between groups or promoting acceptance, giving a poor or good education, processing youngsters like so much raw material or treating them as vital individuals with creative power—the character of the school is all up to the parents. For no community, no matter what its size, can operate a school system of which the parents disapprove, unless those parents are so disinterested and so indolent that they let the whole thing be run for them.

As it is, most schools fall far short of the desired goal of effectiveness. They are usually content to follow the prescribed routine as languidly as possible, and the teaching is, in most large communities, of a very uninspired order indeed. Parents who are particularly interested in education and discover the mediocrity of their schools are more than likely to make every sort of sacrifice to send their youngsters to a private school. As they withdraw their children, they withdraw a great deal of their interest, which leaves the public school system to rock along as best it can minus the influence and determination of a very valuable part of the community. Parents, logically, say that it is all very well to insist that the public schools are the responsibility of everyone, and that it would be better to keep their children in them while pressing for an improvement; but that this means sacrificing their children's education while a long-time process of reform is undertaken.

The defect in this idea is obvious. The fact that a family does not have a child in the community school is no excuse for withdrawing its interest and influence in helping to determine the policies and practices of that school for others. To do so is not only to be guilty of irresponsibility toward one's community but extremely shortsighted. Everyone, finally, is dependent upon the kind of society in which he lives and that society will be only as good as its individual members make it. It is consequently to everyone's advantage to participate actively in the affairs of the schools. If they did, it is probable that we would see a considerable change in the way things are running.

The school has now to be considered more and more an extension of the home. Its very existence is due, in fact, to its assumption of one of the former functions of the home, education. But education about what and for what? We are fond of saying: education for responsible citizenship. But, for the greater part, it is education merely to prepare the youngsters to participate in the industrial society which will ultimately absorb most of them. Schools do not give, as they should, any real education in what it means to be a man or woman or how the life of a man or a woman can be made productive and gratifying. An enormous number of youngsters never go beyond high school. Yet high schools, to a great extent, fail to take account of the fact that this is the last chance these young ones are going to have to extend and deepen their understanding before they are forced to tackle the job of being an adult.

Moreover, schools will have to enlarge their view of their function. Probably, like churches, schools should never be closed. After the routine techniques have been taught, there still remains a wide field of vitally necessary instruction. The use of leisure time, for instance, is a subject that is going to become progressively more important as the inevitable changes in the industrial system lead to shorter work weeks and earlier retirement. The problem of social and recreational life for children in a large city, especially where the parents are working, is one which belongs logically to the schools. Nor should schools serve only the young. Education for adults is becoming of increasing significance, and the schools are the places where it can be best provided. Obviously all this will require an increased staff. But the physical plant is there and the necessary organization available. Also, being as a rule strategically located in relation to community needs, schools should be looked upon as centers for all sorts of educational, recreational, avocational, organizational neighborhood undertakings. But they certainly will not be unless the citizens who pay for them and are ultimately responsible for them make it their business to see that they are.

Unfortunately, the schools will have another job for a long time to come. That is to deal with the problems of the youngsters who in one way or another show signs of inner disturbance. That this need exists is now recognized in a limited way in the guidance and counseling services which are a part, but a decidedly inadequate part, of the school system. As it is, only those youngsters most glaringly out of kilter can be referred to the woefully scanty services, which at present simply are not large enough in terms of a trained staff or physical facilities to do the necessary job.

Teachers also should be trained to act as the first line of defense. They need to know a great deal more about the structure and function of the adolescent psychic equipment in order to deal with the problems that present themselves in every classroom. They are instructed now in ways of maintaining classroom discipline, which they view as a simple problem of "keeping order." But there may be times when "order" is exactly what is not wanted. That, however, is apt to be too subtle a matter for most teachers, who are inclined to view their charges as so many geese being fattened for the slaughter which is graduation. Disorder, of course, is largely the expression of dissatisfaction and discomfort. It is useless to try to "control" it without getting at the basis for it. But to do that requires special insight and understanding. Their training, then, should take that into account, if teachers are to act effectively as the initial officers of the counseling and guidance service. But beyond the efforts of even the best-trained and best-intentioned teachers, there will inevitably be a group of youngsters who require the services of specially skilled guidance and treatment personnel. The schools must be prepared to provide it or the next agencies concerned will be the courts and the mental institutions. None of this in any way is meant to depreciate or disregard the large numbers of devoted and inspired teachers who are, day by day, giving their whole energies to the job.

Since the contacts of the adolescent are by no means confined to school and home, but extend into every part of the city or town, it becomes the responsibility of the whole community to offer these young people the kind of protection and support which they need. For here they expect to find (and properly so) the fulfillment of all their constantly expanding requirements: social, religious, recreational, economic. In a large city special facilities and arrangements are necessary to deal with this problem. There are innumerable agencies and institutions whose major focus is on the needs of young people. These include the Y.M. and Y.W.C.A., the Boy and Girl Scouts, church organizations for young people, community houses, parks and playgrounds activities, and the special programs for youngsters provided by the museums of any city.

One might imagine that everything is there and the young have only to avail themselves of it. To a certain extent this is true, but the network is not well enough organized to prevent an enormous number of youngsters from falling through the gaps. Many of them have to be sought out and the existence of the available facilities brought to their attention. Why should not the school regularly devote some of the time each week to helping these youngsters make plans for the best and happiest use of their week-end leisure? At such times, the various organizations of the community could send representatives to tell the youngsters what is offered and to answer their questions about what they can expect. All activity would finally have to be co-ordinated under an over-all council—a Youth Council—which should be made up of representatives from the proposed neighborhood groups described earlier in this chapter and from the many organizations, institutions, and agencies concerned with the interests of young people. The council would operate as a clearing house and a co-ordinating and planning bureau to see that all facilities and information about them were made available to the entire community.

There will be many, and the author is one of them, who deplore the necessity for all this organization. Aren't we organized enough already? Probably we are overorganized, but you cannot cure the ills of organization by disorganization. The complexities of urban life have grown up willy-nilly. They bear most heavily upon the young and inexperienced, and the consequences of not dealing with them properly can be disastrous. Since we can scarcely expect to demolish our present industrial system overnight, we are obliged to cope with the results of it in the most expeditious and reasonable ways.

There is another area in which the community might well give support, and that is in the matter of jobs and work in general. Here, as we have pointed out earlier, the young are at a particular disadvantage today. We do have regulations determining the age and circumstances under which they can work, but that is the negative side of the story and does nothing whatever to help them toward the immensely valuable experience of work itself. Let no one imagine that we wish to set children to work and undo the immense benefits of the protection these regulations have provided. Furthermore, we recognize the problems of union organization, which cannot allow the inexperienced, temporary and young workers to displace the breadwinners in their ranks. Nevertheless, it is still true that work is part of life; and young people today are the losers in not learning the meaning of responsible work, geared and tempered to their abilities, before they have to face the necessity of actually working for a living. Household chores are no longer the source of experience and pocket money that they once were. By the time a boy or girl reaches fifteen or sixteen, his vacation time has become a real problem—in part, at least, from lack of work.

This seems like a problem that the community might tackle. Certain kinds of work, work as apprentices, seasonal work of all sorts, might be made available. A great many city children, for example, would undoubtedly benefit from going into the country and working in the farm jobs which reach a peak during the summer vacation. Unhappily, all this again would require organization. The Youth Council which has been mentioned could well have as part of its program a clearing house for work suitable for schoolboys and girls in their holiday periods. Most communities teem with needs that could be met by these youngsters if the needs and the youngsters were brought together. Many a housewife, for example, would be happy to turn over the job of going to the laundromat for a few months in the summer to some enterprising boy or girl.

Under proper supervision and with suitable safeguards, there is nothing against work for a strong youngster in his mid-teens and everything in favor of it. Out of such experiences they could get the feel of work, the sense that it is dignified and responsible, the satisfaction of a job done and paid for, the feeling of independence that comes with being able to provide in some small measure for oneself.

One can hear the howls that this idea would evoke from the young themselves and their outraged parents. Are the young and tender to be victimized and thrown to the wolves? Are we to give up all our play and recreation? All work and no play—and so on. But if young people are to learn that work can be a pleasure and a satisfaction, parents are going to have to prepare them for it. This will call for some revision of the way things are now managed in most homes, where little or nothing is expected of the heirs apparent. The point is less what is done or how much than to get across the idea that responsible work is a part of life and not a hideous imposition by someone determined to tear the right to freedom from the reluctant hands of the young.

There are many more ways in which we can and must revise our points of view toward our young people if we are to help them reach their goal of happy and productive maturity. At the center lies the real point, the kind of feeling we have toward them. When we can, as parents, look at them with understanding and without envy, with acceptance of their needs and their inevitable problems, without fear of what they may do to disturb us or to upset our comfortable ways, we will have gone a long way. Now our tendency is to regard the adolescent with a mixture of awe and dread. Our awe comes from the undoubted fact that this is a time of life wonderfully endowed with vision and excitement, with the divine afflatus of the poet, with almost unbounded hope and expectation, and with an energy and drive that are apt to make us gasp with envy. Our dread seems to come from not knowing or being able to predict what they will do with all this driving energy and determination; and from a suspicion that it will not be used to their benefit or our own comfort. There is also a feeling of being powerless to cope with them if they should set off on a course that to us spells disaster.

We need to get back on speaking terms with these young folk and to drop a lot of our superstition about them. They are not mysterious gods and goddesses about to pass a miracle or wreak havoc for the sheer sport of the thing. They are not beyond the reach of reason. They are not natural hoodlums bent upon the destruction of persons or property. They are not people who need to be treated with gloves and given everything they demand. They are not in need of more freedom than anyone else in the world can expect to enjoy. They do not necessarily have to be given the center spotlight in the family life. They are not outside of everything, a group apart and separate.

They can be approached as human beings with a little of the wonderful and a lot of the very unwonderful and quite everyday qualities of all other human beings. They can communicate with anyone who wants to communicate with them. They want to be a part of life and close to their elders. They want freedom, to be sure, but they crave help and strength from their parents in using it well. They can endure the horrid monosyllable "No." They may welcome it and prosper from its judicious use. They are strong and need no special indulgence. They can give as well as take. They have a richness that every family needs and from which it can benefit. It isn't being used to the advantage of the world they live in. They are being made into nonproducers and parasites, which suits them very ill. They really want something quite different from what, in general, they are getting. They want love and understanding above everything else. They want to be able to give it in return. If they fail to get it, they can be very dangerous to themselves and to the society they live in.

They are still special in some ways because they are neither grown up nor entirely children. They are the in-betweens, to themselves as well as to us who watch them. They are inspired with the most intense longing for the life of the grown-up world, but they are afraid of it and cling to the privileges of childhood. They are bewildered as anyone must be in a strange, uncharted land, without guides. They are justified in expecting that those who have been there will give them the benefit of their experience, yet they know that for the most part they must find their way for themselves. They think they know a lot more than they do. That is a good thing, for if they really knew what they had to meet and master, they might show considerably less eagerness to get on with it. Somehow, in all the confusion, they have been let down by the very people to whom they have had to look for guidance. They are reasonably aloof and suspicious, but they are still eager for the help of their elders.

BIBLIOGRAPHY

The following bibliography will give the reader a fairly comprehensive listing of the books the author has consulted—not all of them in their entirety. It does not include any listing of the numerous articles in various scientific journals which have also been covered. Those marked with an asterisk seem to the author to be the ones which the reader may find interesting to consult if he wishes to go further into the subject.

M. F. F.

* AICCHORN, AUGUST. *Wayward Youth* (with a foreword by Sigmund Freud, and a note about the author by the editors.) New York, The Viking Press, 1947.

ALEXANDER, FRANZ, M.D. and STAUB, HUGO (Attorney at Law, Berlin). *The Criminal, the Judge, and the Public.* New York, The Macmillan Company, 1931.

AVERILL, LAWRENCE. *Adolescence.* New York, Houghton Mifflin Company, 1936.

* BLOS, PETER. *The Adolescent Personality.* New York, D. Appleton-Century Co., Inc., 1941.

BUTTERFIELD, OLIVER, PH.D. *Love Problems of Adolescence.* New York, Teachers College, Columbia University, Contributions to Education #768, 1939.

COLE, LUELLA, PH.D. *Psychology of Adolescence.* New York, Farrar, Strauss & Company, 1942.

DUNBAR, H. FLANDERS, M.D., MED. SC.D., PH.D. (Departments of Medicine and Psychiatry, Columbia University). *Emotions and Bodily Changes.* New York, Columbia University Press, 1946.

* EISSLER, K. R., M.D., PH.D. *Searchlights on Delinquency.* New York, International Universities Press, Inc., 1949.

ENGLISH, O. SPURGEON, M.D., and PEARSON, GERALD H. J., M.D. *Common Neuroses of Children and Adults.* New York, W. W. Norton & Co., Inc., 1937.

* FLEMING, C. M., M.A., ED.B., PH.D., F.B., Ps.S. (University of London, Institute of Education). *Adolescence.* London, Routledge & Kegan Paul, Limited, 1948.

FREUD, ANNA. *The Ego and the Mechanisms of Defence*. London, Leonard and Virginia Woolf at the Hogarth Press, 1942.

FREUD, SIGMUND, M.D., LL.D. *Collected Papers*, Vol. 1-5. Edited by Ernest Jones, M.D., Alex and James Strachey, Joan Riviere. London, Hogarth Press, The International Psycho-Analytical Library, 1940-50.

FRIEDLANDER, KATE, M.D. (Berlin). *The Psycho-Analytical Approach to Juvenile Delinquency*. New York, International Universities Press, 1947.

HOCH, PAUL H., M.D., and ZUBIN, JOSEPH, PH.D., editors. *Psychosexual Development in Health and Disease*. New York, Grune & Stratton, 1949.

HOLLINGWORTH, LETA, PH.D. *The Psychology of the Adolescent*. New York, D. Appleton-Century Co., Inc., 1928.

JONES, HAROLD E. *Development in Adolescence*. New York, D. Appleton-Century Co., Inc., 1943.

* MEAD, MARGARET. *Male and Female*. New York, William Morrow & Co.. 1949.

* ———. *From the South Seas*. New York, William Morrow & Co., 1939.

* McPARTLAND, JOHN. *Sex in Our Changing World*. New York, Rinehart & Co., Inc., J. J. Little and Ives Co., 1947.

PARTRIDGE, E. D. (Assistant Professor of Education, New Jersey State Teachers College). *Social Psychology of Adolescence*. New York, Prentice-Hall, Inc., 1938.

PLANT, JAMES S., M.D., Sc.D. *The Envelope*. New York, The Commonwealth Fund, 1950.

RUGGLES, ALLEN M. *These Adolescents—Their Right to Grow Up*. Norman, Oklahoma, Cooperative Book Series 1 #11, 1940.

WHEELER, OLIVE A., D. Sc. *The Adventure of Youth*. London, University of London Press, 1946.

WILLIAMS, FRANKWOOD E., M.D. *Adolescence—Studies in Mental Hygiene*. New York, Farrar, Strauss & Company, 1921-30.

WILLOUGHBY, RAYMOND ROYCE. *Sexuality in the Second Decade*, Vol. II #3, Serial 10. Washington, National Research Council, 1937.

*ZACHRY, CAROLINE. *Emotions and Conduct in Adolescence*. New York, Appleton-Century-Crofts, Inc., 1940.

* *The Adolescent in the Family*. Committee on the Family and Parent Education, Section 3, Education and Training. White House Conference on Child Health and Protection, 1934.

The Forty-third Yearbook of the National Society for the Study of Education. Part 1, Adolescence, 1944. Distributed by Department of Education, University of Chicago.

* *Parents and the Latch Key.* By parents of the children in the Horace Mann Schools. Bureau of Publications, Teachers College, Columbia University, 1936.

Physical and Mental Adolescent Growth. The Proceedings of the Conference on Adolescence, Cleveland, Ohio. Brush Foundation and Western Reserve University.

The Psychoanalytic Study of the Child. Vol. 1-4 (1945, 1946, 1947, 1948). An Annual. International Universities Press, New York.

University of Iowa Studies. Vol. 1 and 2. University of Iowa, Iowa City, Iowa, 1937.

Index

241